The Disciples at the Lord's Table

The Disciples at the Lord's Table

Prayers over Bread and Cup across 150 Years of
Christian Church (Disciples of Christ) Worship

Gerard Moore

☙PICKWICK *Publications* • Eugene, Oregon

THE DISCIPLES AT THE LORD'S TABLE
Prayers over Bread and Cup across 150 Years
of Christian Church (Disciples of Christ) Worship

Copyright © 2015 Gerard Moore. All rights reserved. Except for brief quotations in critical publications or reviews, no part of this book may be reproduced in any manner without prior written permission from the publisher. Write: Permissions. Wipf and Stock Publishers, 199 W. 8th Ave., Suite 3, Eugene, OR 97401.

Pickwick Publications
An Imprint of Wipf and Stock Publishers
199 W. 8th Ave., Suite 3
Eugene, OR 97401

www.wipfandstock.com

ISBN 13: 978-1-4982-0111-7

Cataloguing-in-Publication data:

Moore, Gerard.

    The Disciples at the Lord's table : prayers over bread and cup across 155 years of Christian Church (Disciples of Christ) worship / Gerard Moore.

    x + 106 p. ; 23 cm. Includes bibliographical references.

    ISBN 13: 978-1-4982-0111-7

    1. Disciples of Christ—History. 2. Christian Church (Disciples of Christ)—Doctrines. 3. Christian Church (Disciples of Christ)—Liturgy. I. Title.

BX7325 M65 2015

Manufactured in the U.S.A.   05/04/2015

With thanks to
Gerry Austin OP

and

in memory of
David N. Power OMI

Contents

Preface | ix

1. The Christian Church (Disciples of Christ): Origins and Background | 1
2. The Lord's Supper in the Thinking of Alexander Campbell and the Early Disciples | 11
3. The Lord's Supper in the Manuals of Worship | 30
4. New Influences and Shapes: The Disciples and Ecumenical Eucharistic Convergences | 55
5. The Theology of the Eucharist Expressed in the Communion Prayers | 73
6. Summary and Closing Reflection | 94

Bibliography | 103

Preface

THERE HAVE BEEN ONGOING discussions around worship since the origins of the Christian Church (Disciples of Christ). Its regular Sunday Eucharist, baptismal practices, use of musical instruments, shape of worship, liberty to build services from biblical principles, and the role of ordination have been the touchstones of debate and historical study. And such debates and studies continue. One of the elements that has existed more or less "under the radar" has been the study of what actually has been prayed. This is not an easy element for a free church to work with, given the liberty extended to each congregation to develop its particular forms of worship. Nevertheless, there has been no shortage of manuals, directives, views, and prayer texts on offer to the churches. Across them there has been a degree of consistency that surprises, given the open nature of worship.[1]

In this study I attempt to dig into the manuals and texts that have been part of the furniture of Disciples worship.[2] They reflect something of a Disciples way of eucharistic praying, within which are broad patterns of eucharistic devotion and theology. More recently there have been attempts to bring to Disciples Sunday worship the fruit of the developments and discoveries of the last sixty years of eucharistic scholarship and ecumenical consensus. These can stretch the eucharistic imagination of the Disciples, but also build upon some of the long-time strengths of the church.

---

1. The uniformity of worship across different congregations is also remarked upon by Fikes. See Fikes, "Manner Well Pleasing," 1.

2. Consistent with the practice of the Disciples of Christ, I use the capitalized word *Disciples* either as an adjective or as a noun in possessive case (or in other cases) without an apostrophe.

PREFACE

The following pages are an attempt to map part of this journey. They open with the origins of the church, the eucharistic theology of the early communities, and the influences behind both the foundation of the movement and its eucharistic practices. From this comes a study of selected worship manuals spanning almost a further hundred years of worship.

Though a number of writers and liturgists in the Christian Church (Disciples of Christ) have published collections of prayers for use at the table and have considered what should be in them, there has been little research about the theology of Eucharist as seen from the texts themselves.[3] It is in this area that this study hopes to make a contribution, and so serve elders, ministers, and worshippers in general. One unfortunate aspect of such a close reading of the early sources, however, is the preponderance of masculinist language, whereas inclusive language is now usually found and indeed expected. My apologies in advance for reproducing this language; however, my intention has been to be historically accurate and, where possible, to capture the tenor of the times in which those manuals originated.

There are a number of people who have been decisive in my research and, subsequently, in my writing of the present work. First, I wish to thank Professors David N. Power and Gerard Austin from the Catholic University of America, who were seminal influences and guides both in my original research as part of my licentiate thesis and in the early stages of the writing of this work. My thanks go also to members of the Christian Church (Disciples of Christ) who have prodded me over the years about publishing the results of my research and my discussion of its implications. In particular I would like to single out the Rev. Dr Jessica Cannon, who was a helpful guide and good friend during my licentiate studies, along with fellow Washingtonian the Rev. Laird Thomason, and, more locally, my colleague and friend, the Rev. Denis Nutt, in Sydney. Sole responsibility, for the final text, however, belongs with this author.

—Holy Thursday 2014

---

3. Fikes takes up something of this challenge, concentrating on the hymns sung at the Lord's Supper, however, rather than on the texts for the table. See Fikes, "Manner Well Pleasing," 122–38.

CHAPTER I

The Christian Church (Disciples of Christ)

Origins and Background

THE ORIGINS AND BACKGROUND to the Christian Church (Disciples of Christ) are well-ploughed fields, fertile and interesting.[1] I will review these as a necessary prelude to our closer study of the practices enunciated by Thomas Campbell, the principles underpinning those practices, and the subsequent developments in eucharistic practice across the communities that formed the church. The earliest writings offer a glimpse of the foundations of a new style of Protestantism, marked by the experience of the newly free citizens of the freshly formed United States of America.

THE ORIGINS OF THE DISCIPLES OF CHRIST

A number of movements and approaches lie at the base of the various events that eventually culminated in the formation of the Christian Church (Disciples of Christ). Underlying this development was the general pattern of religious and civil liberty that had become part of the fabric of the new colonies.

---

1. The main sources for this section are Beazley, "Who Are the Disciples?," 17–26, Garrison and DeGroot, *Disciples of Christ*, 21–230, McAllister and Tucker, *Journey*, 19–158, and Harrison, "Sacraments," 94–108. Also helpful with some revision of the impact of the different influences on the original founders of the church is Fikes, "Manner Well Pleasing," 6–46.

Religion in the American Colonies

The colonies, some with an establishment church, became more and more tolerant of dissenting Christian groups, and received from Europe members of different denominations and sects eager to escape the strictures and persecutions there. Despite this tolerance the colonies did not contain a large, actively Christian population, sectarianism did not disappear, nor did denominations reunite.

Attempts were made to evangelize the settlers. The mid-1700s was the period of the (first) "Great Awakening," an evangelistic revival movement. It was Calvinistic, but had appeal across sectarian lines, involving Presbyterians, Congregationalists, and eventually Methodists. It was stronger and more lasting in the southern colonies than in those in the north. By the time of the American Revolution, however, the revival had been spent. The revolutionary fervor brought with it an openness to French philosophy, but not to the exclusion of English thought. In this way the post-revival religious indifference was given impetus with deism and tendencies toward secularization. By the end of the revolution any remaining state churches were disestablished. All denominations were considered equal before the law, and individuals entitled to religious liberty.

A second revival began to take shape at the turn of the nineteenth century, one that would have implications for the beginnings of the Disciples. The main denominations at that time in the United States were the Congregationalists, Episcopalians, Presbyterians, Baptists, and Methodists. Also present were Dutch and German Reformed, French Huguenots, German and Swedish Lutherans, Quakers, and Roman Catholics. Pennsylvania was home to such smaller groups as Moravians, Mennonites, Dunkers, Schwenkfelders, and the Ephrata Society. However on the frontier the main churches were the Presbyterians and Baptists, both strongly Calvinistic, and the Methodists, who were Arminian and revivalistic, and stressed the part emotion played in conversion. An increasing number of believers, in separate groups across the frontier, and, to an extent in the more established areas, were forsaking the restrictions, credal orthodoxies, organizational structures, and clericalism of the denominations and seeking to live and worship simply as "Christians," with the Bible as their guide. Often these groups were unaware of the existence of one another. Often they remained within their denomination until forced out. They were drawn for the most part from the Presbyterians, Baptists, and Methodists; though, dissenting from a number of church practices and teachings, they retained many of the theological concepts of their former denominations. Central to their break with the denominations was their insistence on a right to substitute their individual interpretations of Scripture for those held by the church.

The Christians: Barton Warren Stone (1772–1844)

Among those who became a part of this movement was Barton Warren Stone. Born in America, he was converted to Presbyterianism while studying law at the Greensboro, North Carolina, academy of David Caldwell, himself a Presbyterian minister. Stone had been driven to a despairing search for "saving faith" by a sermon from an evangelistic Presbyterian minister, but found faith only when he heard a much gentler sermon on the love and grace of God delivered by a New Light Presbyterian minister. On conversion he studied for the ministry, and received his license to preach at the age of twenty-four. In 1798 he was ordained.

Stone came into contact with both a number of preachers and ministers who were sympathetic to the ideas of the "Christians," and the revivalism that was sweeping Kentucky at the time with its teaching that salvation was offered for all and not just for the few. He became involved with a group of ministers who together renounced the jurisdiction of the Synod of Kentucky because they held that they were not bound to the Presbyterian Confession of Faith as they had a right to rely on their own individual interpretations of Scripture as the final authority. Against Calvin they held that salvation was open to all. They organized themselves into the independent Springfield (Ohio) Presbytery.

Within months the group issued the "Last Will and Testament of the Springfield Presbytery" (1804), in which they dissolved the presbytery, effectively cutting their links with the Presbyterian Church, and formed a group of "Christians." By the end of the year they had formed at least eight Christian churches in Kentucky and seven in southwest Ohio, mainly from Presbyterian congregations. Each church was independent, but linked through traveling evangelists, and pamphlets and magazines. Any centralization was avoided. From Kentucky the Christian movement spread across the frontier throughout the Middle West. Stone was neither the initiator nor the leader of the fast growing movement. But he was a successful evangelist, teacher, writer, and publisher, and, so gifted, he became the most prominent and influential of the Christians on the frontier.

THE DISCIPLES AT THE LORD'S TABLE

The Disciples

Thomas Campbell (1763–1854)

Meanwhile, in 1807, Thomas Campbell had arrived in the United States from Ireland. His father, originally a Roman Catholic, had become an Anglican. Thomas, however, became a minister in the Anti-Burgher Seceder branch of the Presbyterian Church.[2] He was interested in church unity and had attempted in 1805 to unite the Anti-Burgher and Burgher Seceders in Ireland. This attempt failed, though union was achieved in 1820. In the United States he was appointed to the Presbytery of Chartiers in southwest Pennsylvania.

Difficulties soon arose, however. Two of the most important were his rejection of the use of creeds as terms of communion, and his objection to denying the validity of any coming to faith that was not "saving faith," with its intense experience of emotion. In May 1809, Campbell withdrew from the presbytery and from the Associate Synod of North America. Some months later, in August, he had formed the "Christian Association of Washington" (Pennsylvania), whose aim was for members to work for reform in and through their own churches rather than to form a new church. He wrote its objectives in a short paper, "The Declaration and Address," which the association approved and had printed.

Alexander Campbell (1788–1866)

Thomas Campbell had left his family in Ireland awaiting his summons to meet him when things were settled. On their journey in 1808 they were shipwrecked off the coast of Scotland and forced to spend the year in Glasgow. Alexander Campbell, Thomas' oldest son, spent the year at the University of Glasgow.

In Glasgow, Alexander became involved with the New Scottish Independents, especially Greville Ewing. They were advocating a restoral of primitive Christianity. Independently of his father, Alexander grew away from the Seceder Presbyterian Church, breaking from it before reembarking for the United States. Once there, he joined his father in the Christian Association.

---

2. An explanation of this group is given later in this chapter.

The Brush Run Church

In 1811 the association constituted itself as a church, the Brush Run Church. Thomas Campbell was chosen elder, four deacons were elected, Alexander Campbell was licensed to preach. The next year he was ordained to the ministry. The church held the Lord's Supper weekly and baptism by immersion came to be regarded as essential. This brought the church into closer ties with the Baptists and the church was admitted into the Redstone Baptist Association.

This connection with the Baptists lasted for just over ten years. During that time Alexander Campbell became the dominant figure among the group. He preached in Baptist pulpits, wrote, debated, and began his first magazine, the *Christian Baptist*.[3] He gained a large following in the Baptist congregations, advocating the restoral of primitive Christianity.

Walter Scott (1796–1861)

However the real evangelical thrust of the church came from Walter Scott. He had been born in Scotland, and was a Presbyterian. In the United States he joined a small church that was part of the New Scotch Independent movement. In 1822–23 he met Alexander Campbell. In 1827, Scott became the evangelist for the churches of the Mahoning Association, the Baptist association to which the Brush Run Church and the followers of the Campbells had by now joined.

Scott was not interested in revivalistic enthusiasm nor in distressed and guilt-ridden conversion processes. He preached a simple reasoned formula for salvation. A person must believe upon the clear evidence of the Gospel that Jesus is the Son of God, repent, and be baptized. On accepting baptism, God would fully forgive previous sin, give the Holy Spirit, and grant eternal life.

Scott's preaching was immediately successful. Many joined the church or formed congregations of their own, while other preachers followed his message and method to similar effect.

---

3. A. Campbell edited the magazine for the duration of its publication, from 1823 to 1830. See the bibliography for more publication details.

By 1828, the Mahoning Baptist Association had all but lost its distinctive Baptist character. The association dissolved itself so that the churches could follow the New Testament form of government. No longer Baptists and now joined by people from many other denominations, the churches came to be called Disciples. Though they were all independent and self-governing, Alexander Campbell was clearly the chief intellectual, writer, publisher, and leading figure in the movement. To signify its new status he ceased publishing the *Christian Baptist* and in 1830 began the *Millennial Harbinger*.[4] The millennium of a restored and united Christianity had begun.

The Union of the Disciples and the Christians

Alexander Campbell and Barton Stone had met in 1824. They soon realized how similar their movements were and that the differences between them were not so great as to forbid union. In 1832, the two groups, Stone's "Christians" and Campbell's "Disciples," each made up of autonomous local congregations with no overall hierarchy or structure, decided to unite. Both groups agreed to the restoral of "primitive Christianity." Stone and Campbell used their respective magazines to publicize and solidify the union and both groups accepted Scott's simple evangelism. Converts included members from older churches, and settlers on the frontier who had no affiliations.

At the time of union, church membership was estimated at about 20,000. The church entered a period of strong growth and expansion. By 1860, membership was nearly 200,000. This had grown to 1,150,000 in 1906, but this figure papers over deep rifts that had effectively split the church in all but name. The splinter groups eventually formed the independent Churches of Christ, whose worship does not fall within the scope of the current study.

The Place of Alexander Campbell

Of the four founding fathers, Alexander Campbell is the most prominent in terms of theological output, writing and publishing, and leadership, and serves as the main reference here for Disciples theology and practice. He

---

4. A. Campbell published the *Millennial Harbinger* until 1870. See the bibliography for more publication details.

and Stone were not always in full agreement on issues, but it does no injustice to Stone, Thomas Campbell, or Scott to see Alexander Campbell's writings as representative and formative of the movement as a whole.

THE BACKGROUND TO THE THINKING OF THE EARLY DISCIPLES

Campbell and his fellow workers were part of a confluence of, on the one hand, theological disputes from the "old" world, and, on the other hand, philosophical currents at play across the American democracy, particularly those of John Locke.[5]

Scottish Presbyterianism and the Reformed Tradition

The Reformation background to early Disciples thinking is found in Scottish Presbyterianism and places the Disciples within the Reformed tradition.[6] Thomas Campbell and Stone were ordained Presbyterian ministers. Like Walter Scott, Alexander Campbell was raised in the church, though he had become a Scotch Baptist and follower of John Glas before joining the Disciples. Thus both Calvin and the Westminster Confession are a part of their theological heritage. Alexander Campbell and Scott were also influenced by the sectarian tendencies in Scottish Presbyterianism. Out of the Church of Scotland arose the Seceders, who reacted against the control the aristocracy was gaining over the established church.

In 1733, Ebenezer Erskine and three ministers formed themselves and their parishes into an associate presbytery. They were strong supporters of the Westminster Confession and sought to maintain the doctrine and polity of the Reformed Church. In 1747, this presbytery itself split over the interpretation of an oath requiring magistrates to support the dominance of the Presbyterian Church of Scotland as the established church. The two sects were the Burghers, who signed, and the Anti-Burghers. More divisions occurred. Thomas Campbell was an Anti-Burgher Seceder minister. The causes of such sectarian movements shaped the early Disciples reaction against the intrusion of human authority in religion, while

5. For a discussion of Alexander Campbell as philosopher, see Clanton, *Philosophy*, 11–19.

6. This section is mainly dependent upon DeGroot, *Disciples Thought*, chaps. 12 and 14; Van Kirk, *History*, 60–79; and West, *Alexander Campbell*, 218–22.

the sectarianism itself influenced them to work for the unity of such a fragmented Christianity.

The Scottish Independents also were influential in shaping the Campbell mindset. The first of these, the Old Independents, began with John Glas at the beginning of the eighteenth century. Glas was dissatisfied with any union of church and state, and formed an independent congregation with the aim of restoring the primitive New Testament structures. The Independents interpreted the Scriptures literally, observed the Lord's Supper weekly, and reinstated other apostolic practices such as the love-feasts, the kiss of charity, and foot-washing. Glas' work was taken up by his son-in-law, Robert Sandeman.

A second group of Independents was the Scotch Baptists. They formed in 1767 under the leadership of Archibald McLean. They followed many of the practices of Glas, adding baptism by immersion. We have already noted that Walter Scott was a Scotch Baptist for a while. William Jones of London, who was a frequent correspondent with Alexander Campbell and published some of his works in the British *Millennial Harbinger*, was also a Scotch Baptist.

At the turn of the nineteenth century another independent group arose, the New Independents, led by James and Robert Haldane and Greville Ewing. They had not sought to become an independent church but, as an evangelistic movement, sought only to preach the Gospel. Forced to become a church, Ewing looked to the Old Independents and the Scotch Baptists for guidance, and attempted to reproduce the ideal model found in primitive Christianity. The Lord's Supper became a weekly institution. James Haldane refused to baptize infants and was himself immersed. Though he did not see this as necessary for all the members of the congregation, in effect the church was split.

Ewing became the leader of the paedobaptist group. The split led to the eventual decline of the church. While neither Thomas nor Alexander Campbell belonged to the New Independents, their ideas were current at the time in Scotland and Ireland. Both Campbells had visited the independent congregation at Rich Hill and had come into contact with Ewing. Alexander Campbell acknowledged that he was familiar with the works of Glas, Sandeman, and the Haldanes.

The Philosophy of John Locke

It was John Locke who provided the philosophical basis for early Disciples thought. His writings had been taken up by the Presbyterian moderates of the Scottish school of commonsense realism, especially through its key proponent, Thomas Reid, and were used "to shape a system, both reasonable and moderate, which would avoid the pitfalls of earlier empiricists and appeal to the 'common sense.'"[7]

Alexander Campbell used Locke extensively, especially to understand the relationship between faith and reason. For Locke, and subsequently for Campbell, faith is the assent to a proposition that cannot be reached through the deduction of reason, but comes through revelation from God. The propositions of faith are reasonable in themselves but are beyond the reach of the ability of human reason. Faith, then, cannot contradict reason. Only those things are to be believed in faith that are known to come from God and can be interpreted by reason. Faith rests on testimony, and coming to faith is not to be seen solely in terms of a subjective experience but as acceptance of the testimony along with its moral implications.

Consequently, Campbell and his followers did not urge people to pray for faith but rather "sought to present the gospel, give the divine testimony, and believed that faith must come as a necessity if this course is pursued. Just as the sensible object compels recognition if we open our eyes upon it, evidence compels faith, which is voluntary only in so far as we are able to turn away from the truth."[8]

Once the Bible is established as a book of divine origin,[9] then

> 2. The truths of the Bible are to be received as first principles, not to be tried by our reason, one by one, but to be received as new principles, from which we are to reason as from intuitive principles in any human science.
>
> 3. The terms found in the Bible are to be interpreted and understood in the common acceptation, as reason or use suggests their meaning; but the things taught are to be received not because we

---

7. Pearson, "Faith," 111.
8. Van Kirk, *History*, 62.
9. Locke does this through appealing to miracle and prophecy to authenticate revelation and lay the foundation for faith and morality.

> have proved them by our reason to be truths, but because God has taught them to us.[10]

Thus the Bible is established as a book of facts from which conclusions can be reasoned. It is also established as the only source of revelation.

However, Locke's influence was not limited to Scottish Presbyterianism. His philosophy formed the basis of Thomas Jefferson's thinking, and, in effect, it was the dominant political philosophy in the newly formed United States of America. The people of the frontier, in a new land and away from the old constraints, were predisposed to a message based in the empirical and commonsense framework provided by Locke and developed by Jefferson.[11]

CONCLUSION

It is said that Alexander Campbell traveled everywhere with the Scriptures in one pocket and John Locke in the other. There may be some exaggeration to this, but the movement that he drove brought together the love of Scripture; bible-based theological and liturgical debate; the spirit of the revivals; the philosophical environment nurtured by Locke, Reid, and Jefferson; and the practical nature of living on the frontier of a new world. From this arose a particular approach to Sunday worship based in a weekly Sunday service of the Lord's Supper. It is to this approach that we now turn.

---

10. A. Campbell, *Baptist: Seven Volumes in One*, 380, quoted in Van Kirk, *History*, 65.

11. For the influence of Jefferson and Thomas Reid on the Campbells' preaching in particular, see Casey, "British Ciceronianism."

CHAPTER 2

The Lord's Supper in the Thinking of Alexander Campbell and the Early Disciples

IT IS NOT POSSIBLE to comprehend the currents and directions of Disciples eucharistic thought without a close study of the writings of Alexander Campbell and the influences upon him. His energy and personality, perseverance and optimism were grounded in Presbyterian movements within the Reformed tradition and in the empiricism of John Locke. Campbell's is a "reasoned" approach to the biblical "order of things" at the Lord's table.[1]

WORSHIP AND THE ANCIENT ORDER OF THINGS

Influenced by the Scottish Independent movements, Campbell's concern was to reform the church by bringing it back into line with the "ancient order of things," to bring "the Christianity and the Church of the present day up to the New Testament standard."[2] The earlier Reformers had failed because they had sought to reform creeds and clergy, neither of which, in Campbell's view, belonged to the New Testament:

> Human creeds may be reformed and re-reformed, and be erroneous still, like their authors; but the inspired creed needs no reformation, being, like its author, infallible. The clergy, too, may be reformed from papistical opinions, grimaces, tricks, and dresses, to protestant opinions and ceremonies: and Presbyterian clergy

---

1. For a contemporary overview of Disciples liturgical theology, though without attention to the actual orders of service, see Barclift, "Uniting in Christ."
2. A. Campbell, *Baptist: Seven Volumes in One*, 127.

> may be reformed to Independency, and yet the Pope remains in their heart. They are clergy still and still in need of reformation.³

Put simply, "a restoration of the ancient order of things is all that is necessary to the happiness and usefulness of Christians."

Consequently, Campbell turned to the New Testament for an understanding of worship and found that "there is a divinely authorized order of Christian worship in Christian assemblies and that the worship is uniformly the same, which was to be demonstrated on principles of reason."⁴ Campbell's approach, unlike that of Glas, is not an unmitigated literalism. The Bible contains the facts of God's revelation and they are to be interpreted through reason. Some of these facts act as "first principles" from which conclusions can be deduced. Campbell claims that the Glasites took the principle of apostolic precedent too far with such things as foot washing, the holy kiss, and a set order of service. Campbell's use of reason allows him to interpret the Scriptures and, in the case of worship, enables him to "distinguish between what was their order of worship and manner of edification from what was circumstantial."⁵

Along with Glas and the Scottish Independents, the essential feature of New Testament worship was the meeting of the community on the first day of the week for the breaking of bread:

> From the 2nd [chapter] of the Acts, we learn that the breaking of bread was a stated part of the worship of the disciples in their meetings, and from the 20th we learn that the first day of the week was the stated time for those meetings; and above all we ought to notice that the most prominent object of their meeting was to break bread.⁶

The weekly celebration of the breaking of the bread became the distinctive feature of Disciples worship and much ink was spilled defending it. This defense is based on both the Scriptures and history:

> Thus our seventh proposition is sustained by the explicit declaration of the New Testament, by the reasonableness of the thing itself when suggested by the Apostles, by analogy, by the conclusions of the most eminent reformers, and by the concurrent voice of all

---

3. This passage and the quote in the following sentence are from ibid., 128.
4. Ibid., 166.
5. Ibid., 181.
6. Ibid., 182.

Christian antiquity. But in the plain sayings of the Lord and his Apostles, we rely for authority and instruction upon this and every other Christian institution.[7]

Campbell refers to Justin Martyr, the Council of Antioch, the Council of Agatha in Languedoc, and to Reformers such as Calvin and Wesley to uphold the New Testament ordinance of weekly commemoration of the Lord's Supper. He does not, however, examine or explicitly use either the actual liturgies of those Reformers or the liturgies of the early church. He quotes them mainly to avoid the charge of "innovation." In his mind the witness of the Scriptures is sufficient. From his reading of Acts 2:42 he found what ought to make up worship: "Ought we not, then, to continue steadfast in the breaking of the loaf, and in the teachings of the Apostles, as in the fellowship, as in the prayers commanded by the apostles."[8] However, against Glas, the order was not divinely sanctioned. Campbell rejected any attempt that would make this worship into what he characterized as a "liturgy"—"a ritual form like the Jewish, wholly incompatible with the genius of Christ's religion and [that] would make its meaning and utility to depend essentially on arrangement."[9] Worship was to be free: "Why should we tie up ourselves to formularies of worship when the Lord has left us free as to the time of day or night when, the house or place where, the meeting shall be held . . . whether we shall begin with singing, praying, reading, teaching etc."[10]

ALEXANDER CAMPBELL'S ORDER OF WORSHIP AND THE REFORMED TRADITION

Alexander Campbell was fond of an extract from his Memorandum Book, which described a service that for him was "the nighest approach to the model, which we have in our eye, of good order and Christian decency in celebrating this institution."[11] The order of service is:

[All are seated near the table, which is already furnished]

Call to praise, by the president

7. A. Campbell, *Millennial Harbinger* 1, extra no. 2 (1830) 85.
8. Ibid., 69.
9. A. Campbell, *Millennial Harbinger*, new series, 2 (1838) 247.
10. Ibid., 249.
11. A. Campbell, *Millennial Harbinger* 1, extra no. 2 (1830) 86; also printed in A. Campbell, *Christian System*, 86-88, 342-44.

The Disciples at the Lord's Table

Congregation stands and sings a psalm

Gospel passage on the crucifixion, read by a reader

Prayer of thanksgiving and supplication, by a member of the community

Epistle, read by the president

Song

Invitation to the table

Thanksgiving for the loaf, by the president

Fraction, passing, and eating of the loaf

Thanksgiving for the cup, by the president

Cup passed around

Song

Prayer for the poor and those in ignorance, by a member of the community

Contribution for the poor and the conversion of the world

Period of edification, investigation and inquiry, and singing

Benediction, by the president.

The actual sequence could be varied, but the parts of the service reflect the worship described in Acts 2:42. In effect, the service is a modification of the reformed Directories of Geneva and Westminster. The structure of the 1556 Genevan book adopted by John Knox's congregation is:

Preparation of Bread and Wine—meanwhile singing of a psalm

Words of Institution

Exhortation

Prayer of Thanksgiving

Fraction and Distribution—meanwhile reading of Scriptures

Postcommunion Thanksgiving—Prayer—Psalm 103, or other hymn of thanksgiving

Blessing.¹²

The structure of the eucharistic action in the Westminster Directory of 1645 is similar:

Exhortation

Setting apart of Bread and Wine

Words of Institution (composite Synoptic version or 1 Cor 11:23–27)

[Exhortation on self-examination]

Prayer of Thanksgiving

Fraction and Distribution

Last Exhortation

Thanksgiving

Collection for the poor.¹³

The modifications that are evident in the service described by Campbell model the service more closely on the biblical descriptions of the Last Supper, with its separate thanksgiving and consuming of loaf and cup. The self-examination component of the exhortation is not as strong, though confession of sinfulness may have been included in the thanksgiving prayer as in the thanksgiving prayer in the Westminster Directory.¹⁴ Campbell makes no mention of the words of institution, but they could well have been a part of either the invitation to the table or the thanksgiving prayers for loaf and cup. The service Campbell described is, in a sense, the Reformed order of service "restored" to the ancient order of things.

THE PLACE OF THE LORD'S SUPPER IN THE WORSHIP OF THE LORD'S DAY

Thomas Campbell, Alexander's father, described the form of worship for the Lord's day, placing the Lord's Supper in its worship context. The commemoration of the Lord's death in the Lord's Supper took place as a part of worship on the Lord's day. An hour was spent in singing, praying, and

---

12. Pahl, *Coena Domini I*, 464.
13. Ibid., 468.
14. Ibid.

reading to celebrate the resurrection. This was followed by a period of teaching, edification, and exhortation. After a half-hour break the disciples came together "to commemorate the Lord's death; that all important subject being introduced by singing, then, after reading with pertinent remarks some portion of the sacred record relative to this most sacred and interesting event; and commemorating it as divinely prescribed; having concluded this part of the worship with singing, the teachers might next profitably proceed to review the morning lecture."[15] Following such a review the next week's readings were organized, the group sang and prayed, and on their dismissal each contributed "something to the common stock for religious purposes, as God has prospered him."

Thus the Lord's Supper was one of the ordinances that made up the divine worship, but, as an ordinance, it was virtually independent of the other ordinances. Francis W. Emmons had attempted to show that "it is not in the items themselves alone, but in the items conjointly with the *divine order* of their exhibition that converting power is displayed."[16] In refuting this position, a contemporary, R. Richardson, sheds some light on the relationship between the different parts of worship. The ordinances have not been given a divine order nor do they stand to each other in the relation of cause and effect. Each exercise "is perfect and complete in itself, and equally efficacious in any position, and therefore we do not need any divine law prescribing the order of these exercises for this could add nothing to them and would be perfectly useless."[17] Alexander Campbell also responded to Emmons' concerns, but his disapproval was that an imposed order would not allow for local factors to "be taken into account in the arrangements that are most for edification, sanctification and comfort; which indeed together with our usefulness to the world, are the supreme ends and objects of the Christian Institution."[18]

---

15. This quote and the one in the following sentence are from T. Campbell, *Millennial Harbinger*, new series, 3 (1839) 27.

16. R. Richardson, *Millenial Harbinger* 7 (1836): 296.

17. Ibid.

18. A. Campbell, *Millennial Harbinger*, new series, 2 (1838) 250.

THE DIVINE ORDINANCES

The ordinances are the vehicles of sacrament. The lists of ordinances vary,[19] but they always include baptism, the Lord's day, and the Lord's Supper. Tailored to the reality of human nature, the ordinances contain and impart the grace of God. Calvin Porter has gathered a number of statements from Campbell concerning the ordinances. They are "the mode in which the grace of God acts on human nature," "pregnant institutions filled with the grace of God," "wells of salvation," "the means of our individual enjoyment of the present salvation of God," because "all the wisdom, power, love, mercy, compassion, or *grace of God*, is in the ordinances." Even the Bible is an ordinance: "Not a restoration of the work and the ordinances, as though distant from each other; but simply a restoration of the ordinances; inasmuch as the Bible is one of these ordinances itself."[20] Each ordinance has its own special grace "peculiar to itself; so that no one can be substituted for another, or neglected, without the lack, or loss, of the blessing of the Divine will and grace connected with it."[21] All the ordinances, then, are necessary for good health: "Who can enjoy spiritual life and health without Christ's ordinances and means of Christian health—baptism, and the Lord's Supper, and the other ordinances?"[22] Earlier we saw how both Alexander Campbell and Richardson rejected the notion that there was a divine order associated with the celebration of the ordinances, especially the Lord's Supper, on the Lord's day. In the end, the interrelationship of the ordinances in worship remains unclear.

THE THEOLOGICAL ANTHROPOLOGY UNDERLYING THE DIVINE ORDINANCES

Campbell and the early Disciples displayed more confidence in human nature than the leaders of the Reformation did. Much of the negative anthropology found in the *Apology for the Augsburg Confession* is absent. Though human institutions are not to be trusted, and have led to the obscuring of true worship, sinful human nature is not seen in the Reformation terms of

---

19. Porter, "Thinking Our Way," 307.
20. Ibid., 308.
21. A. Campbell, *Millennial Harbinger*, 5th series (March 1859) 132–33, quoted in Harrison, "Early Disciples," 51.
22. A. Campbell, *Millennial Harbinger*, 4th series (June 1854) 325, quoted in Harrison, "Early Disciples," 52.

its "more serious faults . . . namely, ignoring God, despising him, lacking fear and trust in him, hating his judgement and fleeing it, being angry at him, despairing of his grace, trusting in temporal things, etc."[23] For Melanchthon, because of sin the human person is trapped within a terrified conscience, driven to despair, and can rely only on the promise of forgiveness in Christ for consolation.[24]

Campbell's anthropology is far more positive, set in a different cultural and philosophical environment. The United States was viewed by many living there as "a sort of garden of Eden, where natural man might, at least, have an opportunity to realize the gifts given to him by God, far from the corrupting cultures rooted in the past."[25] The Lockean relationship between faith and reason led to an optimistic assessment of the human person's ability, through reason, to grasp the essentials of faith and live the Christian life. Similar to the way reason both understood the Scriptures and found itself reflected in them, human nature could understand and find its very needs reflected and met in the divine ordinances. The true reformation would come through the restoral of the ancient order of things.

Thus, for Campbell, the ancient institutions take into account the whole person: "The Christian is a *man* . . . the religion of Jesus Christ is a religion for men, for rational, for social, for grateful beings. It has its feasts, its joys and its ecstasies too. The Lord's house is a banqueting place, and the Lord's day is his weekly festival."[26] The Christian institutions are not imposed upon the human person, but shaped for the human person: "None but a master of the human constitution—none but one perfectly skilled in all the animal, intellectual and moral endowments of man, can perfectly adapt an institution to man in reference to all that he is and all that he is to become. Such is the Christian Institution."[27] It is God, and God alone, who truly understands and reveals who the human person is: "The eye of man cannot see itself; the ear of man cannot hear itself; nor the understanding of man discern itself; but there is one who sees the human eye, who hears the human ear, and who discerns the human understanding. He it is who is skilled in revealing man to himself, and himself to man."[28]

23. *Apology for the Augsburg Confession* II, 8, in Tappert, *Book of Concord*, 101.
24. *Apology for the Augsburg Confession* IV, 45, in Tappert, *Book of Concord*, 113.
25. Beazley, "Who Are the Disciples?," 74.
26. A. Campbell, *Baptist: Seven Volumes in One*, 176.
27. A Campbell, *Millennial Harbinger* 1, extra no. 2 (1830) 61.
28. Ibid.

Because the human person is social the Christian institution cannot be simply a private act of piety performed in a group, but is an act of profound fellowship, such that it draws forth from the believer "all that is within him of complaisant affection and feeling, to those joint heirs with him of the grace of eternal life."[29] This affection extends also to "the claims of society at large, as it respects its general improvement, and the amelioration of its conditions." Efforts on behalf of society included foreign Bible associations, temperance associations, and a strong emphasis on universal education "as the best means of promising human happiness, and of preparing the way for the universal spread of the Gospel, and the introduction of that happy era."[30]

Campbell had a certain awareness of the influence of culture on the way a person understood the Christian institution. Americans were more easily able to understand how the concept of the priesthood of the people gave each Christian the capacity to lead in prayer and break the loaf, because "we [Americans] are taught from the cradle that *all power is in the people. The sovereign* people in America can create and they can destroy. With us all officers derive their power from the sovereign people."[31] There was no room, however, for the process of inculturation in early Disciples anthropology. The human person has a nature and the Christian institution has been specifically designed and laid down in the Scriptures to allow that nature to come to God. This is the divine plan. Any obscuring of these designs is to replace authentic Christianity with a human system. It is in this sense that Campbell will differentiate between what is divine and what is human: "It necessarily follows, that Christianity, being a divine institution, there can be nothing human in it; consequently it has nothing to do with the doctrine and commandments of men."[32]

This allows the Disciples to walk the middle road between mere outward formalism in their institutions, on the one hand, and Romanism, on the other. Stone defends the use of forms of worship against an opponent who claims they are merely external, and, as such, are open to abuse by carnal and sensuous minds. For Stone, this is not true of forms sanctioned by divine authority, which must be obeyed: "Praying, singing, the Lord's supper, distributing to the needy, visiting the widow and the fatherless,

---

29. This quote and the one in the following sentence are from ibid., 68–69.
30. A. Campbell, *Millennial Harbinger*, 4th series, 4 (1854) 193.
31. A. Campbell, *Millennial Harbinger* 6 (1835) 80.
32. A. Campbell, *Millennial Harbinger*, 4th series, 4 (1854) 197.

assembling ourselves together to worship, and many others, are all as much 'outward' as baptism, and considered by us as indispensable."[33]

Yet straying from these divinely sanctioned forms is to obscure true Christianity revealed in New Testament simplicity. Doctrines, creeds, and clergy are to be rejected: "Human creeds may be reformed and re-reformed, and be erroneous still, like their authors, but the inspired creed needs no reformation, being, like its author, infallible."[34] The doctrines and creeds of the Roman Church were especially considered in need of reform: "But I have only to offer a *dilemma* to my English brethren who may happen yet to entertain the popish idea of *official grace* still flowing down in a regular sacerdotal stream through all the leaky carcasses of papistic and prelatic priests, from the worm eaten legs of St. Peter's chair, seized with a dry rot seventeen hundred years ago. How grace can emanate from such a putrid carcass would puzzle sages more learned than those of Philistia, dumb stricken by Sampson's riddle."[35]

Though a product of his own culture, Campbell was unaware of the processes of inculturation in the history of Christianity. He saw them as obscuring that true meeting of human and divine that could only take place in those institutions created by the divine and tailored to the exact needs and reality of the human person.

THE MEANING AND CONTEXT OF THE ORDINANCE OF THE LORD'S SUPPER

What is the meaning of the ordinance of the Lord's Supper?[36] It origins are situated in the supper: "We see (Matt. 26:26) that the Lord instituted the bread and wine on a certain occasion as emblematic of his body and of his blood, and as such, commanded his disciples to eat and drink them."[37] The breaking of the loaf and drinking of the cup by the disciples are commemorative of the Lord's death:

---

33. Barton Stone, *Christian Messenger* 13 (1843) 238, quoted in Watkins, "Naive Sacramentalism," 43.

34. A. Campbell, *Baptist: Seven Volumes in One*, 128.

35. A. Campbell, *Millennial Harbinger* 6 (1835) 80.

36. For a challenging overview of this question in Disciples theology, see Hicks, "Churches of Christ."

37. A. Campbell, *Baptist: Seven Volumes in One*, 180.

Upon the loaf and upon the cup of the Lord, in letters which speak not to the eye but to the heart of every disciple is inscribed, "*when this you see, remember me.*" Indeed the Lord says to each disciple when he receives the symbols in his hands, "This is my body broken for *you*. This is my blood shed for *you*." The loaf is thus constituted a representation of his body—first whole then wounded for our sins. The cup is thus constituted a representation of his blood—once his life but now poured out to cleanse us from our sins. To every disciple he says, "For *you* my body was wounded; for *you* my life was taken."[38]

The explicit connection of the loaf and cup to the death of Jesus is through 1 Corinthians 10:16: "This loaf is explained by Paul: 'The *loaf* we break, is it not the communion of the body of Christ.'"[39] Jesus' action of giving thanks with the cup and the bread during the supper becomes, for Campbell, a prayer of thanks for the cup and loaf, which are emblems of Christ's death:

> They [the apostles] received a broken loaf, emblematic of his body once whole, but by his own consent broken for his disciples. In eating it we then remember that the Lord's body was by his own consent broken or wounded for us. Therefore he that gives thanks for the loaf should break it, not as the representative of the Lord but after his example.[40]

Yet the celebration of the Lord's death is also connected with the celebration of the resurrection. Just as the supper is the commemoration of the Lord's death, the celebration of worship on Sunday, the Lord's day, is commemorative of the resurrection. The celebration of the Lord's death was one aspect of the total celebration of the Lord's day, a day devoted to Scripture reading, meditation, prayer, and the ordinances of public worship.[41] For Campbell, the Reformers all agreed "that the celebration of the Lord's supper and Lord's day were inseparably connected; that no Christian community commemorated the resurrection that did not commemorate the sacrifice of the Messiah . . . In fact we cannot have a *Christian week* at all without the *Lord's day* and the *Lord's supper*."[42]

---

38. A. Campbell, *Millennial Harbinger* 1, extra no. 2 (1830) 68.
39. Ibid.
40. Ibid., 67.
41. A. Campbell, *Millennial Harbinger*, 4th series, 4 (1854) 191.
42. A. Campbell, *Millennial Harbinger* 6 (1835) 79.

Campbell chides the Protestant churches for both their infrequent celebration of the supper in face of such a clear mandate for weekly celebration and for their joyless celebration when it is held:

> Whoever heard of a text addressed to prove a monthly, a quarterly, a semi-annual or an annual breaking of the bread . . . some of them make a Mt. Sinai convocation of it. With all the bitterness of sorrow, and gloominess of separation, they convert it into a religious penance accompanied with a morose piety and an awful affliction of soul and body . . . And the only joy exhibited on the occasion is that all is over, for which some of them append a day of thanksgiving.[43]

For Disciples it is a celebration both solemn and joyful:

> It is to him as sacred and solemn as prayer to God, and as joyful as the hope of immortality and eternal life. His hope before God, springing from the death of his Son, is gratefully exhibited and expressed by him in the observance of this institution.

THE ORDINANCE OF THE LORD'S SUPPER AS SACRAMENT

How does the ordinance work? It does not gain any efficacy from the hands of ministers. Campbell is emphatic on the centrality of the priesthood of all believers. He approvingly quotes poet John Milton: "All Christians are a royal priesthood, therefore any believer is competent to act as an ordinary minister according as convenience may require, provided only he be endowed with the necessary gifts, these gifts constituting his commissions."[44] He is equally emphatic that the giving of thanks for loaf and cup by a minister is no different from that by any believer:

> Do you not thank God for the cup while the priest stands by the table and do you not handle the loaf and cup when they come to you? And would not your thanksgiving have been as acceptable if the human mediator had not been there, and your participation as well pleasing to God and consolatory to yourself if you had been

---

43. This quote and the one in the next sentence are from A. Campbell, *Baptist: Seven Volumes in One*, 175.

44. A. Campbell, *Millennial Harbinger* 1, extra no. 2 (1830) 83.

the first that handled the cup or loaf, as when you are the second or fifty-second in order of location?[45]

Ordination to ministry is about overseeing the community and good order: "We are for order—good order in all Christian communities, large and small. Hence no one acts either *pro tempore* as an elder or overseer for a single day, but by the choice or appointment of the brethren."[46]

It is not the bread and cup that are changed but the person who receives them. In this way the occasion of the supper is an effective celebration. In being reminded of the sacrifice of the Savior, the worshipper is filled with the "philanthropy of God," strengthened in faith, and the heart is "cheered" with the love of God.[47] The ordinance appeals to the senses and is effective when it reaches the heart of the believer now opened to further grasp the reality and depth of the promises of salvation in Christ. It presents the facts of faith and allows them to be experienced: "[Christians] must perceive, realize, appropriate, and feel the *blood* of Christ *applied* to our reason, our conscience, our will, and to our affections."[48]

To not wish to partake of such spiritual food is indicative "of a want of spiritual health, or of the presence of a moral disease, which, if not healed, must issue in apostasy from the Living Head."[49]

The worshipper is called into a new relationship with the other disciples: "Each disciple in handing the symbols to his fellow disciples, says, in effect, 'You my brother, once an alien, are now a citizen of heaven . . . You have owned my Lord as your Lord, my people as your People. Under Jesus the Messiah we are one.'"[50]

The activity of God underlies the ordinance. Its strength comes from the power of the cross and its authority from Jesus' own command. It is God who has laid the banquet and invited the disciples to the feast. It takes place on the Lord's day, in the Lord's house, at the Lord's table. Campbell emphasizes this point when urging Christians to convene weekly around the Lord's table: "Much more in accordance with the genius of our religion would it be to see them oversolicitous to be honored with a seat at the King's

---

45. Ibid., 65.
46. A. Campbell, *Millennial Harbinger* 6 (1835) 80.
47. Ibid.
48. A. Campbell, *Millennial Harbinger*, 4th series, 5 (1855) 662, quoted in Harrison, "Early Disciples," 53.
49. A. Campbell, *Millennial Harbinger* 1, extra no. 2 (1830) 86.
50. Ibid., 68.

table, and asking with intense interest might they be permitted so often to eat in his presence and in honor of his love."[51] At the table there is communion in Christ: "As 'God in Christ' is one personality, so all Christians—or those in Christ, are the *one body* of which he is *the head*."[52]

Campbell's understanding of the Lord's Supper belongs within the Reformed interpretation. The Presbyterian critique of the early Disciples did not find fault with them with regard to interpretation of the Eucharist, and Campbell and Richardson claim that they do not differ from Protestants in general in the nature and design of the ordinance.[53] Specifically Reformed emphases are in the significance given to the fraction, the spiritual presence of Christ, and the concepts of spiritual nourishment and spiritual graces being conveyed through sensible realities such as bread and wine.[54] The influence of Locke is apparent in the importance given to knowledge that comes through the senses, and how the sacraments appeal to the rational mind as well as to the heart. This allows Campbell's concept of Eucharist to be subjective without being overly pietistic.

"STYLE" AND "MANNER" IN WORSHIP

Two aspects of the Lord's Supper that necessarily received much attention were the style and manner in which worship was carried out, and the use of symbolic actions. Gathering frequently at the Lord's table was not sufficient: "Much depends on the *manner* of celebrating the supper as well as upon the *frequency*." The way worship is carried out affects the worshipper's ability to take part in it: "While there is the form of doing everything, there is all attention to the thing signified." Campbell is not simply against sanctimoniousness and pharisaism. There exists a Christian simplicity: "The well-bred Christian is like the well-bred gentleman—his manners are graceful, easy, artless and simple." Not surprisingly, simplicity is a very part of worship: "The simplicity of the Christian worship runs through every part of it."[55] Good order and Christian decency result in fitting worship, worship in which "everything exhibited the power of godliness as well

---

51. Ibid., 86.
52. A. Campbell, *Millennial Harbinger*, 5th series, 1 (1858) 216.
53. Harrison, "Early Disciples," 71–72.
54. Ibid.
55. The quotes in this paragraph up to here are all from A. Campbell, *Millennial Harbinger* 1, extra no. 2 (1830) 86.

as the form; and no person could attend to all that passed without being edified and convinced that the Spirit of God was there."[56] Christian decency and Christian manners are the result of constant prayer and meditation upon salvation.[57]

However, simplicity of worship is not just the fruit of prayer. It is a characteristic of New Testament worship and its loss is related to apostasy. According to Richardson, "the apostasy from primitive Christianity is undoubtedly characterized as much by a departure from the simple and significant acts of public worship attended to by the first Christians, as by its substitution of human opinions for the Gospel of Christ."[58] Only in simple worship can the heart be moved: "By means of a few simple facts, commemorated by its institutions, it influences the human heart to love... The actions which it prompts, like those dictated by nature, proceed from the heart, and are equally unconstrained and unaffected."[59] Anything that goes beyond this simplicity is both of human invention and inimical to true Christianity: "Systems and theories, indeed, ordinances, sacraments, and ceremonies of human inventions have been the bane of Christianity."[60]

SYMBOLS AND SYMBOLISM IN WORSHIP

Simplicity of style allows the symbols in the service to have an effect on the worshipper. They act as symbols in the way they present the "simple facts" of faith to the heart of the believer and influence the heart to love. Perhaps the most immediate symbolism is in the name "the breaking of the bread." Campbell rejected both "Eucharist" and "sacrament" because they were of human origin and so went against his Reformation thrust of calling biblical things by biblical names.

In fact the breaking of the bread became known as the Lord's Supper. Campbell spends time justifying this. Was it really a supper? "But as the Lord had eaten a religious supper, had partaken of the paschal lamb with his disciples, before he instituted the breaking of the loaf and the drinking of the cup as commemorative of his death, it seems improper to call it a

---

56. Ibid., 88.
57. Ibid., 86.
58. R. Richardson, *Millenial Harbinger* 7 (1836) 295.
59. Ibid., 296.
60. Ibid., 297.

supper for it was instituted and eaten *after a supper*."[61] However "supper" is used in the New Testament figuratively as well as literally, and so "if we say in accordance with the Apostles' style, the Lord's day, the Lord's table, the Lord's cup, we may also say the Lord's supper."[62]

However, Campbell is not consistent in his use of biblical terminology. He introduces the nonbiblical term "emblem" to describe and explain the real significance and spiritual reality of the earthly realities used in worship, but he does not give a precise definition of "emblem" or "emblematic." He uses "emblem" and its cognates in a number of circumstances, though most often to describe the symbolic reality of the bread and wine. His usage often means either resemblance to a spiritual reality or reminder of a spiritual reality. The twelve loaves that were placed in the temple were an "emblem of the abundance of spiritual food in the presence of God for all who dwell in the holy place." The light from the seven lamps on the golden candlestick was "emblematic of the perfect light not derived from this world." The Christian house of God he described as the "emblematic house of God."[63] Campbell's most central emblems are the bread and wine: "While he participates in the symbolic loaf, he shows his faith in and his life upon, the Bread of Life. While he tastes the emblematic cup, he remembers the new covenant confirmed by the blood of the Lord."[64] The emblematic reality of the bread and wine does not come from the power or authority of a minister: "We regard the loaf and cup as receiving no *virtue* from *official* hands, nor more useful or holy to him that received it first from the bishop's or deacon's hands, than it is to him who receives it last from the hands of the humblest brother or sister in the Lord's family."[65] These emblems are powerful in worship because they originate in Scripture, are part of the divine ordinances, and are able to influence the mind and heart to remember what God has done.

The ways in which the bread and cup are presented and passed on are also highly symbolic. For Campbell, the loaf must be whole, symbolizing the oneness of the congregation: "As there is but one literal body and but one mystical or figurative body having many members; so there must be but one

---

61. A. Campbell, *Millennial Harbinger* 1, extra no. 2 (1830) 66.
62. Ibid., 67.
63. All the quotes in this paragraph up to here are from ibid., 63.
64. A. Campbell, *Baptist: Seven Volumes in One*, 175.
65. A. Campbell, *Millennial Harbinger* 6 (1835) 80.

loaf. The Apostle insists upon this, 1 Cor. 17 'Because there is the one loaf, we, the many, are one body; for we are all partakers of that one loaf.'"[66]

If the unity of the loaf signifies the oneness of the church with and in Christ, the fraction of the loaf signifies something quite different. The breaking of the bread signifies Christ's death for us: "They [the apostles] received a broken loaf, emblematic of his body once whole, but by his own consent broken for his disciples. In eating it we then remember that the Lord's body was by his own consent broken or wounded for us. Therefore he that gives thanks for the loaf should break it, not as the representative of the Lord, but after his example."[67]

Both passing the emblems and receiving the emblems are symbolic. To pass the bread and cup to another is to say "you my brother, once an alien, are now a citizen of heaven . . . under Jesus, the Messiah, we are one" and to receive the bread and cup is to say "Lord I believe it. My life springs from your suffering; my joy from your sorrows; and my hope of glory everlasting from your humiliation and abasement unto death."[68]

By keeping the style simple, the early Disciples believed that the symbols were able to directly influence the heart to love more deeply, and that more elaborate liturgies and theologies only obscured such a process.

PASTORAL NORMS REGARDING THE LORD'S SUPPER

Who may approach the Lord's table? Who can participate in the ordinances? These questions can be seen both in terms of the personal worthiness of the believer, and in terms of whether a person is either to be admitted as a believer or disqualified as a nonbeliever.

Even though the Campbell–Stone movement arose partly from a deep dissatisfaction with the sectarianism of the church communities in the United States, the question of who could belong was not easily settled. Campbell believed that only adults baptized by immersion were truly baptized and able to partake of the Lord's Supper. Stone, himself an immersionist, disagreed: "I have found nothing in scripture to forbid me to commune with unbaptized [i.e. unimmersed] persons at the Lord's table."[69]

66. A. Campbell, *Millennial Harbinger* 1, extra no. 2 (1830) 64.
67. Ibid., 67.
68. Both quoted passages in this paragraph are from ibid., 68.
69. Barton Stone, *Christian Messenger* 4, pp. 236–37, quoted in Sikes, "Worship

Campbell's response was based on the lack of a specific ordinance allowing it: "It is not enough to say there is not a command or precedent for it . . . If there is not a command or precedent for it we can easily find one against it. Because whatever is not commanded by the Lord is will worship and . . . obnoxious to the curse."[70]

The question underlying the opposing viewpoints was never settled and was related to the controversies surrounding the validity of nonimmersion baptism and the validity of the baptism of children. Amongst the more liberal-minded Disciples a somewhat irenic position emerged. Isaac Everett states: "We are compelled . . . to recognize as Christians many who have been in error on baptism, but who in the *spirit* of obedience are Christian indeed." Consequently all cannot be excluded from the Lord's table. It is left for the Lord to bring people to the table: "Our practice . . . is *neither to invite nor reject* particular classes of persons, but to spread the table in the name of the Lord, for the Lord's people, and allow all to come who will, each on his own responsibility."[71]

The open communion debate dealt with scriptural qualifications for coming to the Lord's table. The other area that must be looked at is that of the personal worthiness of the members of the congregation in relation to taking communion. Campbell was acutely aware of many Christians' fear of eating and drinking unworthily. He quotes John Wesley: "They are so much afraid of *eating and drinking unworthily*, that they never think how much greater the danger is, when they do not eat or drink at all."[72] Wesley's answer was to show that Paul was not referring to communicants' personal unworthiness but the unworthy way in which the Corinthian community was holding the supper.[73]

Campbell's own approach is different. Taking the example of the "common priests" of the Old Testament, he notes how they did not fear to approach the golden table in the temple, to place the loaves upon it, nor to take and eat that bread. All Christians, however, belong to a much greater priesthood, the royal priesthood of Christ, and so should have no fear

---

among Disciples," 21.

70. A. Campbell, *Millennial Harbinger* 1 (1830) 473–74, quoted in Sikes, "Worship among Disciples," 21.

71. Both quotes in this paragraph are from Isaac Everett, *Millennial Harbinger*, 5th series (1861) 711, quoted in Sikes, "Worship among Disciples," 25–26.

72. A. Campbell, *Millennial Harbinger* 1, extra no. 2 (1830) 82.

73. Ibid., 82.

in approaching the table: "I trust it is apparent that the royal priesthood may approach the Lord's table *without fear*, inasmuch as they are consecrated to officiate by a blood far superior to that which consecrated the fleshly priesthood."[74] The table was not a place of judgment but a place of healing and feasting.

CONCLUSION

Alexander Campbell and the early Disciples arose out of the Reformed tradition as interpreted by Scottish Presbyterianism and the Scottish Independent movements. Philosophically they were grounded in the empiricism of John Locke. Reason and reasonableness always featured in their thinking. Their principal concern was to restore Christianity to the "ancient order of things," to the order and structure of the New Testament community in Acts. The Lord's Supper, one of the divinely sanctioned ordinances, was held weekly as part of the worship on the Lord's day. Liturgically the supper was based on the liturgies of Geneva and Westminster, but "restored" to reflect the more normative New Testament worship. Theologically their interpretation of the meaning of the supper remained within the Reformed tradition, with its emphasis on the priesthood of all believers, the spiritual presence of Christ, denial of any change to the bread and wine, and the importance of communion. The respect for reason engendered by Locke balanced the revivalist enthusiasm and pietism current at the time.

---

74. Ibid., 65.

CHAPTER 3

The Lord's Supper in the Manuals of Worship

As the Disciples moved into the second half of the nineteenth century, their worship changed. The change was not in theological concepts or constructs but in style and manner. These changes were inevitable, but not without considerable friction and division. Campbell and the early Disciples had failed to see that the simplicity of worship that they attributed to the New Testament ordinances was the simplicity of the pioneer culture in which they lived and in which they felt deeply at home. As culture changed, so did the Disciples manner of worship. The "typical" church of the 1860s still had about it the feel of the frontier:

> The congregation gathered in a plain, rude, unadorned building devoid of all symbolism. At one end of the building stood the pulpit, perhaps on a platform slightly raised above the floor level. In many cases the pulpit stood between the two front doors of the building. Although the custom changed across the years, the two doors were provided initially because men and women sat on different sides of the building. Rough wooden benches or pews provided little enough comfort to minimize temptation to slumber through the service.[1]

Yet by the 1920s this was no longer the norm. Organs had been introduced, along with specialist choirs; the common cup was replaced with individual cups; new hymnals appeared without any mechanism for authorizing them; churches were designed by architects; and there arose concern for suitable furnishings, hangings, and symbols. The Lord's day was made up of two services. In the morning was the communion service, while the

---

1. Adams, "Worship among Disciples," 34.

THE LORD'S SUPPER IN THE MANUALS OF WORSHIP

evening service was evangelistic, which was more in keeping with revivalism than pentecostalism. The desire to be faithful to the teaching of the New Testament remained, alongside a continuing distrust of Romanism. Moses Lard combines these characteristics in an extreme form in dealing with the growing use of organs in Disciples churches:

> Let us agree to admit organs, and soon the pious, the meek, the peace-loving, will abandon us; and our churches will become gay worldly things, literal Noah's arks, full of clean and unclean beasts. To all this let us add a few volumes of inner-light speculation, and a cargo or two of reverend dandies dubbed pastors, and we may congratulate ourselves on having completed the trip in a wonderfully short time. We can now take rooms in Rome, and chuckle over the fact that we are as orthodox as the rankest heretic in the land.[2]

Perhaps the most far-reaching developments of this period were the printing of worship manuals for use by ministers and for the planning of services. The early Disciples had valued spontaneous prayer because it was unaffected and straight from the heart. They would write about the order of service and the contents of worship but not so much the contents of the actual prayers. In this sense the worship was "free," that is, not prescribed. In effect the development of planned liturgies using either manuals or a mimeographed order of service was not removing this freedom but "was replacing a simple habitual tendency to reproduce an order of service which had become traditional, and also was replacing the tendency to order worship according to the spontaneous promptings of spirit."[3] The manuals are important sources for Disciples thought, and are the direct forerunner of Osborn's *Christian Worship: A Service Book*.[4] The acceptance by congregations of more formalized worship led to the stabilization and development of liturgical forms, and a much broader and ultimately more open understanding of liturgy. It also dampened the tendencies toward revivalism and pentecostalism in the Disciples, keeping them within the Reformed tradition.[5]

---

2. Moses Lard, *Lard's Quarterly*, April 1865, quoted in Adams, "Worship among Disciples," 44.

3. Blakemore, "Disciples of Christ, 1920–1966," 56.

4. This was first published in 1953; see the bibliography for more publication details. Henceforth referred to as *Christian Worship*.

5. Osborn, *Christian Worship*, 57.

For the rest of this chapter we will examine the understandings of the Lord's Supper that emerge from these manuals. However, given the sizeable number of manuals till the publishing of Osborn's manual,[6] we will examine only a selection: in particular, two early manuals, those of Foy (1889) and Garrison (1891), as well as a somewhat later one, that of Cave (1918).[7] These three afford a look at the development of the structure of worship both for Sunday morning worship and for the service of the Lord's Supper, and provide the context subsequently for Osborn's order of service. After examining these early manuals, we will study the manual by Ainslie and Armstrong (1923),[8] which, while providing a structure for the services, shows a movement away from the restorationist ideal and a desire for a more contemporary form of worship. Abbott's subsequent book of 1926,[9] reprinted many times over the next quarter of a century, provides a large number of thanksgiving prayers that can be examined for both their structure and their theology. Perhaps the most important contribution of Abbott's book, though, is the way it allows the minister to develop an integrated service around a single theme. This is one of the strengths of Osborn's manual, too. Related to this is the development, through the manuals, of a calendar. Each manual has different features and content, so direct comparison across them all is not possible. However, a compelling picture of Disciples worship emerges when they are viewed as a whole.[10]

FOY'S *CHRISTIAN WORKER* (1889)

In 1889 Jos H. Foy published *The Christian Worker: A Practical Manual for Preachers and Church Officials*. It contained services, sermon outlines, Scripture passages, and prayers for a variety of situations and events.

---

6. Unfortunately there appears to be no register of worship resources.

7. Foy, *Christian Worker*; Garrison, *Alone with God*; Cave, *Manual for Ministers*. See the bibliography for fuller details.

8. Ainslie and Armstrong, *Book of Christian Worship*. See the bibliography for fuller details.

9. Abbott, *At the Master's Table*. See the bibliography for fuller details.

10. Other worship books and manuals consulted but not discussed here include Lockhart, *Ministry*; Smith, *Manual of Forms*; Humbert, *Worship and the Devotional Life*; Green, *Minister's Manual*; Lapin, *Communion Manual*; and DeForest Murch, *Christian Minister's Manual*.

The Order of Service

Foy gives an "Order of Worship" for the Lord's day, noting that each congregation should conduct its worship in a regular order, though there is no prescribed order. For morning worship he suggests:

1. Invocation
2. Hymn, of which one stanza may be read
3. Scripture lesson, [which] can be read responsively
4. Hymn
5. Prayer
6. Collection
7. Announcements
8. Sermon
9. Hymn
10. Benediction, [which] is to permit strangers and non-members to retire if they prefer to do so
11. Communion
12. Doxology
13. Benediction.[11]

Evening worship is the same as morning except the communion, doxology, and second benediction are omitted. Preaching is allocated the bulk of the time spent in worship: thirty to forty-five minutes.

The communion is dealt with in its own chapter. Though no precise order of service is given, the chapter contains:

- The accounts of the Last Supper: Matt 26:26–28; Mark 14:22–26; Luke 22:19–22; and 1 Cor 11:23–26
- Devotional excerpta for the supper
- Fraction of the loaf and the placing of pieces on a plate, by the minister
- Pouring of wine into goblets
- Communion

---

11. Foy, *Christian Worker*, 128–29.

- Outlines for talks at the communion service
- Conclusion by a doxology or a suitable hymn, and a benediction.

Some further comments can be made. The talks at the communion service would come at the beginning of the service, presumably if there was no minister available to preach a sermon. The devotional excerpta could have been used as models for the prayer, or prayers, of thanksgiving over the bread and wine. They closely resemble most later thanksgiving prayers. It is not stated whether communion in the bread followed the blessing of the loaf or whether communion in cup and loaf took place together. The service is clearly in line with the order praised by Alexander Campbell and dependent on the directories of Geneva and Westminster, which were discussed earlier.

The Structure and Content of the Devotional Excerpta

Given that these early sources are beyond the reach of most readers, the devotional excerpta for the supper will be given here, with an analysis to follow.

I.

We do not presume to come to this thy table, O merciful Lord, trusting in our own righteousness, but in thy manifold and great mercies. We are not worthy so much as to gather up the crumbs under thy table. But thou are the same Lord whose property is always to have mercy; grant us, therefore, gracious Lord, to eat and drink as discerning the Lord's death, that our souls may be washed through his most precious blood, and that we may evermore dwell in him and he in us. Amen.

II.

We glorify thy holy name, Almighty God our Heavenly Father, because, of they tender mercy, thou didst give thine only Son, Jesus Christ, to suffer death upon the cross for our redemption, making a full, perfect and sufficient sacrifice for the sins of the whole world; and we thank thee sincerely that he did institute and command us in his holy Gospel to continue to observe this Supper in perpetual memory of that his precious death and sacrifice until he should come again. We pray that as we partake of this perishing bread we may in faith feed upon Him who is the true bread of life, the bread that came down from heaven, and that we may go hence, strengthened by thy Spirit in the inner man. We ask it in Christ's name. Amen.

III.

Our Lord, our God, we are worms of the dust, defiled with tendencies to sin and actual sin, busy with folly and too careless of eternity. But we come to thee in faith and beg to be received into the compassionate arms of thy mercy. Cleanse our hearts, strengthen our faith, enliven our hopes, give us victory over sin and perfect us in love, patience, humility and obedience. Be present to illuminate, comfort and refresh they people while they partake of this wine with grateful and contrite hearts. May their hearts be sprinkled afresh with the blood that calls for mercy and forgiveness as they taste the emblem of that blood which was shed for many for the remission of sins. We ask these things in Christ's dear name. Amen.

IV.

Encouraged by these memorials, dear Lord, we come to thee as straying sheep to their shepherd; as the sick to their physician, and as condemned criminals to a merciful and powerful intercessor. Nay, more, we come as thy children, feeling their weakness, yet confident of thy strength; realizing their coldness and half-heartedness, yet believing in thy readiness to impart thyself to them and to lift up drooping heads and hands. O thou who didst take upon thyself for love of us the infirmities of our nature, give us of thy Spirit that we may be exalted spiritually and feel that heaven is our home. From the ample provisions of the Gospel, of which this is a lively memorial, may we derive support, strength, armor and defense. Let this cup of blessing be to us the communion of the blood of Christ, let the bread be the communion of the body of Christ. May they not only stir up our pure minds by way of remembrance, but as we partake in faith, may strength and wisdom from above enter into our souls, so that henceforth we may bear about with us continually the dying of the Lord Jesus. And may the consecrated life of Jesus also be manifested in our mortal bodies here dedicated anew to thee. Hear us for Jesus' sake. Amen.[12]

---

12. Ibid., 89–90.

The structure and theological content of the devotional excerpta show a reworking of the Scottish Presbyterian tradition. The prayers are addressed to God the Father, though Prayer IV begins addressing Christ, but by the end it is addressing the Father. They are basically prayers of petition. Only Prayer II has an explicit thanksgiving, while Prayer III mentions the worshippers' "grateful and contrite hearts." Prayers I and IV have no thanksgiving. Prayers I, III, and IV have a confession of unworthiness along with an assurance of mercy. In Prayers II and IV the Spirit is called down upon the worshippers for inner strength and spiritual help. The Spirit is not called down upon the elements. All the prayers stress the importance of communion in that it is in partaking that the worshipper discerns the Lord's body. The notion of petition is dominant, including petition to eat and drink as discerning the Lord's death, to dwell in Christ, to be strengthened by the Spirit, and to be cleansed and spiritually refreshed in Christ. These features, though not always included in each prayer, resemble the themes found in the prayer of thanksgiving in the Westminster Directory— the confession of the sinful state of humanity, praise for the redemption from that state, prayer for the availability of that redemption through the means of grace, adhesion to Christ alone in faith through the Spirit, and prayer for the work of the Spirit in the communicants and the elements to effect spiritual union.[13] The brevity of the excerpta does not allow for any expansion on the themes. However a major difference from the Scottish Presbyterian prayers is that the excerpta place much less importance on the work of the Spirit in both communicants and elements.

There are two examples of more direct dependence on the Scottish Presbyterian tradition. Prayer I is simply an economical paraphrase of the Humble Access and *epiclesis* in the prayer of thanksgiving in the communion service of the Draft Liturgy of 1618.[14] The prayers said by the minister while breaking the loaf and pouring the wine are also lifted directly from the Draft Liturgy.[15] The structure and contents of a great number of the thanksgiving prayers published up until the publication of *Thankful Praise* in 1987 follow the structure and contents of these devotional excerpta. This highlights the strong dependence of the Disciples on the Reformed tradition of worship.

---

13. Pahl, *Coena Domini I*, 468.
14. Ibid., 482.
15. Ibid., 484–85.

The Theology of Eucharist

The five outlines for talks at the communion service contain a somewhat comprehensive theology of the Eucharist, showing elements from the Restoration ideals and from Reformed theology. The Lord's Supper is a memorial and a thanksgiving. It is a thanksgiving for the atonement won by Christ: "It reminds us that the claims of moral government have been fully met. That the salvation accomplished by Jesus is a completed one from the side of heaven, and that if we appropriate that finished salvation God is pledged to sustain us in the saved life."[16]

The supper is not a merely formal ceremony—"We do not approach these emblems of the broken body and shed blood of our Lord and master carelessly, irreverently, ceremonially"[17]—but a ceremony that brings awareness of Christ's spiritual presence: "And while this ordinance brings to us vividly the fact of the Lord's absence in his glorified body, it also suggests to us his spiritual presence and helpfulness, and his coming again to gather up his jewels. 'Do this in remembrance of Me'—not of Me as a dead fact stranded on the shores of the oblivious ages, but of Me as a warm, living, loving presence in the midst of sincere worshippers in all the ages."[18]

The memorial is communal: "It is a communion with God in Christ, and with one another";[19] transformative: "See the sacred use of common things. The bread and wine represent the body and blood of God's dear Son. Let our lives and our callings be transfigured likewise";[20] and eschatological: "It is a prophecy of a second coming 'without sin unto salvation.'"[21]

The symbols act as symbols in that they call to mind what Christ has done and the community's connection with the Christian community in Acts. They include the reading of the Last Supper narratives; the cup "that symbolizes his finished work for our salvation"; the distribution of the emblems, symbolizing "that no Christian man must live unto himself or for himself"; the table spread, representing the banquet of salvation to which the believer is invited; and the bread and wine, representing (1) the body and blood of Christ, (2) the sacred use of common things, and (3) sheer

---

16. Ibid., 93.
17. Ibid., 94.
18. Ibid.
19. Ibid., 96.
20. Ibid., 95.
21. Ibid., 96.

gratuity: as gifts, they remind the believers that "salvation, like the bread and wine, is God's gift."[22] The action of the deacons in distributing the communion symbolized the deacons in Acts 6:2–3, who served the tables in the Christian assembly.[23] This allowed the congregation to represent directly that body of early Christians as they gathered around the apostles and came together at the Lord's table on the Lord's day.

The communion service is a complete action in itself, with its own focus—the death of Christ—and its own set of symbols. It is independent of the earlier parts of the worship service. This is highlighted on examination of the ordination ceremonies for elder and deacon. Both ministries entail roles in the supper yet the Lord's Supper is only a part of the service if the ordinations are held during the morning service.[24]

Foy incorporates an awareness of personal sin and relates it to the communion. Though there is no act of communal confession, the devotional excerpta contain admission of sin and subsequent confessions of faith. The acknowledgment of personal sin actually makes one a "fit partaker" for "if you know that you are not what you ought to be, but long to be better than now are, gratefully eat and drink the emblems; for in recognizing that you are a sinner and need a savior, and will need him all your journey through, you do discern the Lord's body."[25]

A Church Calendar

The manual also shows signs of the development of a calendar relating the worship of the Lord's day, though not necessarily the Lord's Supper, to communal events. It is concerned mainly with the sermon. Thanksgiving Day is to be happily and openly celebrated. Easter Sunday can also be kept as a special feast, though it is "purely of human origin" and "timorous eyes" may see in it "an encroaching ecclesiasticism."[26] Special collection days also have their impact on the organization of worship. They should be either noted in the church directory, or placed on a list "pasted in every hymnal."[27]

---

22. All quoted passages in this sentence are from ibid., 95.
23. Ibid., 37.
24. Ibid., 126, 127.
25. Ibid., 92–93.
26. Ibid.
27. Ibid., 130.

GARRISON'S *ALONE WITH GOD* (1891)

In 1891 J. H. Garrison published *Alone with God: A Manual of Devotions*. It contains a series of meditation and prayer forms for private devotions, family worship, and special occasions. There is no order of worship; however, private prayers in preparation for communion are given in the section on private devotions, while the Lord's Supper is dealt with in the section on special occasions.

The Structure of the Thanksgiving Prayers

Two prayers for use before communion are given, as well as two prayers for thanksgiving for the loaf and two for the cup. The prayers of thanksgiving at the Lord's table are:

> For the Loaf I
>
> Almighty God, our heavenly Father, in approaching this Thy table, we would come in the spirit of true humility, feeling our unworthiness and confession our sins. We presume not to sit down with Thee at this communion, because we are worthy of that fellowship to which Thou dost graciously invite us. But we come trusting in Thy unfailing mercy manifested by the sacrifice which we now commemorate. We thank Thee for this loaf, emblem of the broken body of Jesus. Help us to receive it with reverence and love. As we eat of this bread may we do so in loving memory of him who was bruised for our iniquities, and by whose chastisement we are healed. Grant, O Father, that we may feed daily on the true Bread which came down from heaven, and so grow constantly in his image; for Christ's sake. Amen!

> For the Loaf II
>
> Gracious God, our heavenly Father, we thank Thee for a place in Thy church and among Thy people. We thank Thee for this institution of our Lord's own appointing which he has asked us to observe in memory of him. We pray Thy blessing upon us while we draw nigh to Thee in this sacred ordinance. As we feed upon this bread, help us to remember that Christ is the true Bread which came down from heaven, and that in him alone can the hunger of our souls be satisfied. Enable us, by faith, to feed on this life-giving truth and grace, until we shall grow into his likeness, and share at last in his glory. We ask this in his precious name. Amen!

The Disciples at the Lord's Table

For the Cup I

We thank Thee, O our heavenly Father, that Thou didst so love the world as to give Thine only begotten Son, that whosoever believeth on him might not perish, but have everlasting life. We thank Thee, dear Lord, for that great love which brought Thee to the earth, and caused Thee to lay down Thy precious life for us. As we partake of this fruit of the vine in memory of Thee and of Thy great sacrifice in our behalf, cause the tragic scenes of Gethsemane and of Calvary to pass before our minds. May Thy deep humiliation so affect our hearts, that all pride, and vanity and undue love for earthly things may be banished from us, while we look at the cross. May we walk in fellowship with Thee here, all our days, and be permitted at last to drink this cup anew with Thee in Thine everlasting kingdom where we will praise Thee and Thy redeeming grace forever. Amen!

For the Cup II

We thank Thee, O Lord, for this cup of blessing which speaks to us, in symbolic language, of the precious blood of Christ shed for the remission of our sins. We thank Thee for this privilege of manifesting our faith in, and our love for our risen and glorified Savior. As we drink of this emblematic cup, may the vision of the cross rise before us, with all its unspeakable shame and agony, until we realize in some measure the debt of gratitude we owe to Him who became obedient unto death that we might have eternal life. May we be drawn closer to Thee and closer to one another in holy love and fellowship, through our joint participation in this solemn feast. Through the blood of the everlasting covenant, emblemized by this wine, cleanse us, we pray Thee from all unfaithfulness, and bring us at last to join in ascriptions of praise to him who hath washed us from our sins in his own blood, to who be glory forever and ever. Amen![28]

The thanksgiving prayers are similar to the excerpta in Foy. They begin with an address to the Father, and contain thanksgiving, petition, and acknowledgment of sinfulness, with an assurance of forgiveness. Thanksgiving is given a much stronger emphasis in these prayers than in those of Foy. Though the first prayer for the loaf opens with the idea of the worshipper's humility and unworthiness before making thanksgiving, the other three prayers all open with thanksgiving. In the first prayer for the

---

28. Garrison, *Alone with God*, 225–26.

loaf, thanksgiving is made for the loaf, which is a reminder of the cross: "we thank Thee for this loaf, emblem of the broken body of Jesus."[29] In the second, it is made for membership in the church: "we thank thee for a place in Thy church and among Thy people"; and for the supper as a Christian institution: "we thank Thee for this institution of our Lord's own appointing."[30] In the first prayer for the cup, thanksgiving is made for the incarnation, and for the sacrifice on Calvary: "we thank Thee, dear Lord, for that great love which brought Thee to the earth, and caused Thee to lay down Thy precious life for us."[31] The second prayer over the cup offers thanks for the supper as a Christian institution: "we thank Thee for this privilege of manifesting our faith in, and our love for, our risen and glorified Savior."[32]

In Foy, however, there is no thanksgiving in Devotional Excerpta I and IV, and in III it is restricted to the statement, "while they partake of this wine with grateful and contrite hearts."[33] In II, God is glorified because "Thou didst give thine only Son, Jesus Christ, to suffer death upon the cross for our redemption," and God is thanked for instituting the Lord's Supper: "we thank thee sincerely that he did institute and command us in his holy Gospel to continue to observe this Supper."[34]

Petition remains important in Garrison. It is mainly for help in "remembering" Christ, for personal cleansing, and for fellowship with God both here on earth and in the everlasting kingdom. There is a further diminution of the role of the Spirit, who is neither invoked on the communicants nor on the elements, nor even mentioned.

The Theology of Eucharist

The theology in these thanksgiving and devotional prayers is much the same as that found in Foy but with more emphasis given to the image of feasting. The supper is described as a "sacred ordinance which we are to observe in memory of Thee."[35] The prayers make clear that the communion service is a memorial. It is "the memorial feast of the Lord's supper, in memory

29. Ibid., 225.
30. Ibid.
31. Ibid., 226.
32. Ibid., 227.
33. Foy, *Christian Worker*, 89–90.
34. Ibid., 89.
35. Garrison, *Alone with God*, 163.

of Christ who gave himself as ransom for us."[36] The loaf is the "emblem of the broken body of Jesus,"[37] while the cup "speaks to us in symbolic language of the precious blood of Christ, shed for the remission of our sins."[38] Memorial is used in the sense of recalling to the mind. In the first prayer of thanksgiving for the cup, addressed to Jesus, it says: "As we partake of the fruit of the vine in memory of Thee and Thy great sacrifice, cause the tragic scenes of Gethsemane and Calvary to pass before our minds."[39] The second prayer, addressed to the Father, has the same concept of memorial: "As we drink of this emblematic cup, may the vision of the cross rise before us, with all of its unspeakable shame and agony, until we realize, in some measure, the debt of gratitude we owe to Him."[40] The emblems are symbols that help the mind to realize the reality of what God has done. This way of keeping memorial is also effective in that it is able to bring a sense of the spiritual presence of Christ and strength in Christ: "Give us, we beseech Thee, a realizing sense of Thy spiritual presence with us in this institution, that we may each be strengthened thereby."[41]

The dominant image for interpreting the supper is that of feasting. It is a "solemn yet joyful feast," a "memorial feast of the Lord's supper."[42] Its effects are seen in terms of nourishment: "Feed our souls upon the Bread of Life. Quench our thirst with the Water of the River of Life."[43] The loaf and cup are emblematic not just in being placed on the Lord's table but essentially in being consumed: "As we feed upon the bread, help us to remember," "As we partake of this fruit of the vine . . . cause."[44] The eschatological implications of the supper are also in the image of feasting: "And grant us at last the unspeakable joy of sitting down together, with the innumerable company of the redeemed, at the Marriage Supper of the Lamb in Thy everlasting kingdom."[45]

36. Ibid.
37. Ibid., 225.
38. Ibid., 227.
39. Ibid., 226.
40. Ibid., 227.
41. Ibid., 224.
42. Ibid., 163.
43. Ibid., 223.
44. Ibid., 226.
45. Ibid., 224.

CAVE'S *MANUAL FOR MINISTERS* (1918)

In 1918 R. C. Cave published *A Manual for Ministers*. He describes it as "largely a compilation" of the works of others along with his own, always with the intention of preserving the thoughts of each author.[46] He provides a form for the communion service, to be conducted by either a minister of the Gospel or an elder, "for use when the communion is the main part of the service, as often is the case in country churches."[47] The text shows a tension between the place of the sermon and the place of the Lord's Supper, with the sermon winning out: "When much of the time for worship is taken up by a sermon, the form may be shortened."[48]

The Order of Service

The order of service is as follows:

1. Hymn
2. A short introductory talk on the institution and design of the Lord's Supper
3. Prayer of preparation, with responses by the congregation
4. Uncovering of the emblems
5. Call to self-examination
6. Paraphrase of the scriptural warrant (minister)
7. Prayer of thanks for the bread (elder)
8. Breaking of the bread (minister)
9. Distribution of the bread (deacons)
10. Scriptural warrant for the cup (minister)
11. Thanksgiving for the cup (elder)
12. Distribution of the cups (deacons)
13. Recovering of any remaining emblems (deacons)
14. Prayer of praise, with responses by the congregation

---

46. Cave, *Manual for Ministers*, 5.
47. Ibid., 48.
48. Ibid.

The Disciples at the Lord's Table

15. Hymn

16. Benediction

The prayer of preparation with responses asks God to cleanse the hearts of the believers so that they may experience spiritual communion with the Lord in the supper. There are two prayers of thanksgiving, one each for cup and loaf:

> We bless thee, merciful Father, for every revelation of thyself which thou hast graciously vouchsafed to us; but especially do we now thank thee for the wondrous revelation of thy Son, and for this bread, which is designed to bring afresh to our remembrance his body as it was bruised and broken on the cross for us. May we eat of it discerningly, gratefully, and lovingly, communing in spirit with him who so loved us and sacrificed himself for us; and, as we eat, may our hearts become more loving and our lives be consecrated anew to thy service, through Jesus Christ, our Lord. Amen.
>
> Our Father who art in heaven, we give thee unfeigned thanks for this symbolic cup of which we are privileged to drink in remembrance of our Lord and Savior Jesus Christ, who endured the agony of crucifixion, and poured out his blood, that we might be delivered from bondage to sin, come into the enjoyment of peace with thee, and have the blessed hope of life everlasting at thy right hand. As we drink of this cup, and contemplate his amazing sacrifice of himself for us, may our hearts glow with a love for him that will cleanse them from all ungodly desires and affections, and make them temples of holiness, swept and garnished and dedicated to thee, unto whom belongeth "the kingdom, and the power, and the glory, for ever." Amen.[49]

These prayers contain the same elements as those in Foy and Garrison: address to the Father; thanksgiving; petition, especially for partaking with discernment; and admission of sinfulness, with an assurance of forgiveness. Thanksgiving is the prominent theme in the two prayers. It is given for redemption in Jesus: "for the wondrous revelation of thy love given unto us by thy son"; and for his having instituted the Lord's Supper itself: "we now thank thee . . . for this bread, which is designed to bring afresh to our remembrance,"[50] "we give thee unfeigned thanks for this symbolic cup of which we are privileged to drink in remembrance."[51]

---

49. Cave, *Manual for Ministers*, 57–60.
50. Ibid., 58.
51. Ibid., 59.

Petition is made so that the worshipper may discern the Lord's presence with gratitude: "may we eat of it discerningly, gratefully, and lovingly";[52] and for further conversion, cleansing, and dedication: "may our hearts become more loving and our lives be consecrated anew to thy service,"[53] "may our hearts glow with a love for him that will cleanse them form all ungodly desires."[54]

There is no invocation of the Spirit.

The structure of the service is a slight variation of the Scottish Reformed tradition. Cave's manual, however, does show the roles the elders play in the service. As we have noted already, a minister or an elder could lead the service but it is the role of the elder to make the prayer of thanksgiving. This was the role given to the elders by the apostles.[55] It reflects the Disciples stance against clericalism, their quest for restoration to the apostolic structures, and their desire to enable each community to celebrate the Lord's Supper independently of the availability of an ordained minister.

Cave attempts to include the congregation actively in the worship through the use of responsive prayers. Thus prior to the uncovering of the emblems there is a responsive prayer of preparation led by the minister or elder.[56] Immediately following the serving of the cups by the deacons there is a responsive prayer of praise.[57]

The Theology of Eucharist

With regard to the theology of the Eucharist the manual reflects what we have already seen. In the first introductory talk on the Lord's Supper, it is described "as a most sacred institution; and it has been termed the 'culminating point,' the 'holy of holies' of Christian worship."[58] Yet its relationship to the other parts of Sunday worship is not clear. It is held in some tension with the importance of the sermon, and is not related at all to the services

---

52. Ibid., 58.
53. Ibid.
54. Ibid., 59.
55. In the ceremony for the ordination of an elder, Cave writes: "It was their charge to direct public worship, to administer the sacraments." Ibid., 29.
56. Ibid., 56.
57. Ibid., 60.
58. Ibid., 50.

of ordination.[59] Its purpose is to be "a commemoration of the atoning death of our Lord Jesus Christ, in which his disciples, remembering that all are one with him, should forget all differences of wealth, station, ability and attainment, and coming together as one divine family united by brotherly love, should gratefully commune in spirit with the Lord."[60] As a commemoration, it draws the worshippers to focus on what Christ has done for them: "We must put out of view all worldly concerns, dismiss from our minds and hearts everything that may tend to make our mental vision of the Lord less clear and distinct, and concentrate our thoughts upon him whose body was broken and blood was shed."[61]

Since for Cave "we become morally like that on which we meditate,"[62] the emblems do not work on only the mind of the worshipper, but, in working on the worshippers' minds, they work to "awaken in our hearts an answering love that will cleanse us from all evil, and make us one with Christ and the Father in thought, desire, affection, and purpose."[63] The emblems have no value in themselves: "These symbols are of no value, save as they quicken the remembrance and lead to the contemplation of that which they symbolize."[64] Thus at the end of communion any emblems left are simply re-covered with the cloth. The emphasis here is not so much on the metaphor of feasting but on the positive and rational anthropology of the Disciples, the ability of the believer to understand the symbols, and the fact that the symbols themselves have been designed precisely for humans: "They are graciously designed to arrest and counteract the worldly influences that tend to make us forgetful of our 'holy calling.' "[65]

Some of the symbolisms seen earlier are retained, others changed. The symbolism of the one loaf is not used. Instead, the bread is "broken beforehand into as many pieces as may be required,"[66] yet the fraction of a piece of bread by the minister is retained for its symbolic value. The deacons pass out the elements. The ceremony for the ordination of deacons gives this a

---

59. Ibid., 16–40.
60. Ibid., 50.
61. Ibid., 51.
62. Ibid., 52.
63. Ibid., 55.
64. Ibid., 51.
65. Ibid., 50.
66. Ibid., 58.

strong symbolic value. A part of their duty is "serving the tables,"[67] which is associated with their ministry to the table and their ministry to others. When the minister lays his hands on the deacons' heads, the minister prays that Christ may say of them, "Come ye blessed of my Father . . . In as much as ye have done it unto one of the least of my brethren, ye have done it unto me."[68] As the deacons serve the congregation, they are seen as other Christs and their service as service to Christ. These symbolic gestures work to bring to the mind and heart the gift of salvation wrought by the death of Christ.

AINSLIE AND ARMSTRONG'S *BOOK OF CHRISTIAN WORSHIP* (1923)

A Book of Christian Worship, prepared by Peter Ainslie and H. C. Armstrong, was published in 1923 for voluntary use amongst Disciples. It had a broad ecumenical flavor. Going beyond the Disciples own tradition, it "incorporated those methods of worship which have been found most helpful through the centuries from the beginning of spiritual worship to the present time."[69] It encouraged Christians to attend Sunday services in other churches from time to time.[70]

The Order of Service

The worship book provides a general order of service for worship, an order of service for Sunday worship, and two orders of service for the communion service: a full order and a brief order. The general order of service for worship is almost exactly that given by Foy. It is made up of:

1. Call to worship

2. Hymn of praise

3. Responsive reading of a psalm

4. Scripture lesson

5. General prayer

---

67. Ibid., 36.
68. Ibid., 39.
69. Ainslie and Armstrong, *Book of Christian Worship*, 3.
70. Ibid., 26.

6. Hymn, anthem, or solo
7. Announcements
8. The offering
9. Hymn
10. Sermon
11. Hymn of invitation and consecration
12. Communion of the Lord's Supper
13. Benediction

The order for the communion service parallels those given earlier. The service is:

1. Invitation to communion, by minister
2. Communion scripture lesson, by minister
3. Prayer of penitence and confession, by minister
4. Lord's Prayer, by all the people
5. Psalm 23, by all the people
6. Prayer of thanksgiving over the loaf, by minister or another proper officer
7. Communion in the loaf
8. Prayer of thanksgiving over the wine, by minister or another proper officer
9. Communion in the wine
10. Prayer of thanksgiving, a responsive prayer with minister and people, as well as a prayer by the minister
11. Blessing
12. Doxology
13. Benediction

A number of responsive prayers have been added, as well as a prayer of penitence and confession, the Lord's Prayer, and Psalm 23. The prayers over loaf and cup are as follows:

> Our Father, we thank Thee for Thy great love manifested to us because Thou hast sent Thy son Jesus Christ into the world that we might live through Him. Grant us grace, we beseech Thee, that as He gave His body to be broken for us we may present our bodies a living sacrifice, which is our reasonable service. Cleanse our hearts, we pray, and enable us to eat of this Bread in gratitude and love, discerning the Lord's body, in the Name of Christ. *Amen.*
>
> We thank Thee, O God, for the love of Christ who loved us and gave Himself for us on the Cross. Help us, we pray, that seeing Him lifted up we may be drawn to Him in faith and obedience. Help us to take up our cross and follow Him, realizing that we are not our own, but that we are bought with a price even the price of the Cross. Grant us Thy grace, we beseech Thee, that we may drink of this cup worthily, and may the blood of Christ cleanse us from all sin, in the Name of Christ. *Amen.*[71]

These prayers of thanksgiving follow the customary format, being addressed to the Father and made up of thanksgiving for the crucifixion and petition so that, in their partaking, the people may discern the Lord's body. They do not contain a confession of unworthiness and assurance of pardon, presumably because of the prayer of penitence and confession. The communion Scripture lessons are either 1 Corinthians 11:23–29, Matthew 26:26–29, or Luke 22:14–22. Scripture is used extensively throughout the service.

The Theology of Worship

Though the service is very much within the Disciples tradition, theologically and structurally it indicates some new emphases in the understanding and practice of worship. Instead of Campbell's insistence on returning to the "ancient order of things," Ainslie and Armstrong sought to fashion a contemporary worship that endeavored "to speak in terms of the present day experience."[72] The order of service was prepared with "the highest ideals and principles of church worship in view," with due regard for the "different moods of devotion, aspiration, adoration, penitence and confession, thanksgiving and petition, consecration and edification."[73]

---

71. Ibid., 31–32.
72. Ibid., 3.
73. Ibid., 3–4.

Principles of posture have been used also. Though none of these necessarily opposes Campbell's basing worship on the forms of the ancient ordinances, they give a broader perspective to the liturgy as a single action, and open the way for a more integrated relationship between Sunday worship and the Lord's Supper. The communion of the Lord's Supper should be "made the crowning part of the Sunday Morning Service," and to show forth its importance "the Communion Table should occupy the most exalted place in the church."[74]

It is appropriate to hold the Lord's Supper on other occasions, "such as at the opening of a convention, the first evening of an evangelistic meeting, family reunions and Thursday evening preceding Easter."[75] Worship is given further context through the development of a liturgical calendar. A table, given before the contents page, lists the dates of Easter from 1923 till the year 2021. The contents page lists the special days, both religious and civil.[76] However there are no specific prayers for inclusion in the Lord's Supper on special days.

Altogether the manual shows a stronger interdependence between worship, the Lord's Supper, and the religious and social events in people's lives, while making an attempt to bring about a contemporary form of worship.

The Theology of Eucharist

There are also some theological variations and innovations in the manual. There is no symbolism of the fraction, but there is the symbolism of all communing at the same time, and "in order to preserve the ancient symbolism of the communion cup the flagon may be retained and placed on the Table between the trays containing the individual cups."[77] The prayer of thanksgiving is not specifically for the bread and cup, but "for Thy great love manifested to us"[78] and "for the love of Christ who loved us and gave Himself for us on the Cross."[79]

---

74. Ibid., 28.

75. Ibid.

76. These are Christmas Day, the Lenten Season, Easter Sunday, Ascension Day, Pentecost Sunday, Education Day, Bible Sunday, Children's Day, Citizenship Sunday, Labor Day, Rally Day, and Thanksgiving Day.

77. Ibid., 28.

78. Ibid., 31.

79. Ibid., 32.

There is also the notion of offering sacrifice. Usually sacrifice refers to that of Jesus on the cross. This is the notion present in Foy: "to suffer death upon the cross for our redemption, making a full, perfect and sufficient sacrifice for the sins of the whole world";[80] in Garrison: "As we partake of this fruit of the vine in memory of Thee and of Thy great sacrifice on our behalf";[81] and in Cave: "As we drink of this cup . . . and contemplate his amazing sacrifice of himself for us."[82] However in the prayer of thanksgiving over the bread, the leader prays that "we may present our bodies a living sacrifice, which is our reasonable service."[83] These notions of sacrifice and thanksgiving, though more attuned to the broader Christian eucharistic heritage, were not, however, integrated into later manuals.

ABBOTT'S *AT THE MASTER'S TABLE* (1925)

First published in 1925, Abbott's manual was subtitled "A Book for Those Who Participate in the Rite of the Eternal Atonement." The book does not provide an order of worship; rather it presents themes for use at the Lord's Supper. For each theme there is a hymn, a short Scripture text, a meditation, and a separate thanksgiving prayer for loaf and cup, each with an accompanying Scripture verse.

The Thanksgiving Prayers

There are fifty-five pairs of thanksgiving prayers—too many to reproduce here. They follow the already familiar structure in that they are addressed to the Father, and contain thanksgiving and petition. The one and only reference to the Spirit in all of the prayers is for the Spirit to renew the worshippers.[84] Some of the prayers have a confession of unworthiness and assurance of forgiveness. In most of the prayers thanksgiving and petition are central, though thanksgiving seems to be more prominent than petition.

---

80. Foy, *Christian Worker*, 89.
81. Garrison, *Alone with God*, 226.
82. Cave, *Manual for Ministers*, 59.
83. Ibid., 31.
84. Abbott, *Master's Table*, 136.

In the prayer for the loaf in the prayers for a New Year communion,[85] thanks is given for the ordinance of the Lord's Supper, thanks that "there is a place and an hour of escape from the exhausting, deadening power of the world." Petition is for "a fresh experience of Thy goodness and mercy as we eat of this loaf," and to "waken us to deeper love and greater effort in Thy kingdom." However, the prayer for the cup contains only thanksgiving.

In the two prayers for the Easter communion,[86] thanksgiving for the loaf is for the redemption through Christ's death. There are prayers of petition for worshippers to discern "the Lord's body broken for us," for deeper faith, for repentance, and for strength "to live in the life he gives." Again, the prayer for the cup contains only thanksgiving.

But this is not always the case. The two prayers for the theme "Experience Transfigured"[87] are mainly prayers of petition, with little thanksgiving. Generally, though, thanksgiving is the more prominent element.

The Theology of Eucharist

The theology of the Eucharist is that of the Reformed tradition, Alexander Campbell, and the other manuals that we have examined. To come to the Lord's table is to participate in an act that brings great comfort, fellowship, and perspective:

> To sit at the Table is a rest beside a river ... It is the influence of the Upper Room that has followed the Church through all the ages, keeping it true to the Great Heart which broke to redeem it. It brings to men and women of today, weary, heavy laden, embattled by sin, and humiliated by faults and imperfection, the comforts of a spiritual Galilee, the inspiration of the mystic Olivet which forever looks forward with unclouded vision to new, vast, radiant horizons from the mountain top.[88]

This comfort and strength come through the symbols of bread and wine, blessed at the Lord's table, raising the mind to further consciousness of what Christ has done for the believer by his death. In a prayer for the cup, the elder prays: "We lift up our hearts and exalt our souls in the

---

85. Ibid., 15–16.
86. Ibid., 99.
87. Ibid., 164.
88. Ibid., 3.

consciousness that Jesus was born into the world to save us from our sins and that he died on the cross."[89] Such remembering has an effect on the worshipper.

In the meditation for the New Year communion, it says, "The vision at the Lord's Table of the suffering Christ renews courage, quickens love."[90] Not to remember is to lose the source of Christian strength: "To forget him is to lose the one great inspiring example of life, to let go our chief strength . . . Vision and memory work wonders of beauty and miracles of peace in those who practice the Lord's Table."[91]

A Thematic Approach to Worship

What is most important about Abbott's book is that it provides a large number of themes to commemorate the Lord's death and to reflect on the life of the Christian. There are fifty-five themes, some seasonal—Christmas, New Year, Easter; others occasional—"Why the Good Suffer," "The Taste of Heaven," "The Supper and Christian Union." As we have seen, for each theme there is a hymn, a Scripture text, a meditation, and a separate thanksgiving prayer for loaf and cup, each with an accompanying Scripture verse.

An example of this integration of the Lord's death and Christian life, in this case, singing, is "The Song at the Lord's Table."[92] The text is Mark 14:26. The meditation relates this theme specifically to the Lord's passion: "So there is something sweet and wonderful in the Lord's supper because it inspires to songs in the night . . . How could my master sing when faced with such deep and awful experiences as Gethsemane."[93]

The prayers of thanksgiving for loaf and cup attempt to unify the theme with thanksgiving for Christ's death for sins:

> We are able to sing songs in the night because Thou dost love us and because Jesus died on the cross to save us. Today, also, O God, we may sing a new song. The old things have died away and the

---

89. Ibid., 216.
90. Ibid., 15.
91. Ibid., 127.
92. Ibid., 57.
93. Ibid., 58.

new floods of light and love, and power, and purpose have poured into our hearts. Our song, gracious God is a song of deliverance.[94]

Because no order of service is suggested, these prayers are not fitted into the context of the worship on the Lord's day. However they enable a minister to combine Scriptures, a sermon, and a communion service as an integrated whole around one of the themes. Thus we see how, in Abbott, the Lord's Supper is still a commemoration of Christ's death, but it is placed in a broader perspective, and allows the supper to be integrated more fully into a total worship context.

CONCLUSION

The development and use of manuals stabilized Disciples worship and allowed it to develop. Worship that was planned allowed for more variety and freedom than worship that was simply spontaneous. The structure of the worship in the manuals is close to that of the Reformed tradition, as is the theology found in the prayers, sermon outlines, and directions. There is some diversity amongst the manuals, mainly connected with the use of symbols and changes in "style" in worship. The use of thematic liturgies brought more integration to the service as a whole, as did the development of a calendar. The themes may or may not have been linked to calendar events such as Easter or Thanksgiving, but there was no sense of a liturgical calendar around which worship was planned. Given the importance of the sermon and the fixed theme of the Lord's Supper as a commemoration of the crucifixion, the thematic approach was more important. In view of the underdeveloped quality of the calendar and the resistance to it,[95] the thematic approach was also more acceptable within the Disciples tradition. By 1925 neither the ideal of restorationism nor the philosophical presuppositions of John Locke were viable foundations for theology or worship. New foundations were needed to uphold a way of worshipping that had, by now, become traditional amongst Disciples communities.

---

94. Ibid., 60.
95. See Foy, *Christian Worker*, 92.

CHAPTER 4

New Influences and Shapes

The Disciples and Ecumenical Eucharistic Convergences

BY THE LATE TWENTIETH century an ecumenical consensus was developing around questions concerning the Lord's Supper. The Disciples theology, customs, and practices were not in step with many of the findings of scholarship and their incorporation into contemporary worship. They were not alone in this, but it seemed as if a church that had held to the biblical understanding of the Sunday service of the Lord's table had lost ground and distinctiveness.

In this chapter and the following one, I will explore the Disciples response to this dilemma, a response that is ongoing. To do this, I will contrast the first 150 years of worship with the possibilities and challenges at play in more recent ecumenical and scholarly discoveries. The accumulation of early wisdom is best exemplified in G. Edwin Osborn's highly popular manual *Christian Worship: A Service Book*, while a revised vision is seen in Keith Watkins *Thankful Praise* (1987). By no means is either text seen as an end point, but rather they are intriguing *starting* points in a heightened ecumenical journey. We begin with a close look at the contents of Osborn's manual.

OSBORN'S *CHRISTIAN WORSHIP* (1953)

Christian Worship contains orders of service for a number of worship occasions, as well as "compilations of related Scripture sentences and of prayers, both classic and modern, arranged under more than 100 topics."[1] The final part of the book contains an extensive topical index, with each topic cross-referenced, and a lectionary of New Testament and Psalm readings. The components that make up the order of worship in each service are set out in relation to a general pattern of worship. For Osborn, during each act of worship a definite cycle is followed in the consciousness of the worshipper. This cycle is recognizable and forms a pattern. The most satisfactory worship is achieved by conforming the order of worship to this pattern.[2] This concept of a pattern for worship, though, will be discussed in the next chapter. It is mentioned here so as to show its relationship to the order of service. Each order of service is divided into four movements, which, combined, make up the pattern for worship. These movements are (1) an act of reverence, (2) an act of fellowship, (3) an act of dedication, and (4) an act of renewal.

The Order of Service for Sunday Morning Worship

The manual provides an order of service for Sunday morning worship and an independent order for the communion of the Lord's Supper. The Sunday morning order of worship is as follows:

Act of Reverence:

1. Organ Prelude
2. Choral Call to Worship
3. Period of Silent Prayer
4. Processional Hymn
5. Introit
6. Gloria Patri [can substitute an hymn of adoration]
7. Unison Prayer of Invocation

Act of Fellowship:

8. Period of Silent Prayer
9. Anthem or Solo

---

1. Osborn, *Christian Worship*, v.
2. Ibid., 3.

NEW INFLUENCES AND SHAPES

10. Announcements
11. Scripture Lesson
12. Choral Response of Praise
13. Pastoral Prayer
14. Choral Prayer Response

Act of Dedication:

15. Hymn of Affirmation or of Consecration
16. The Offering
17. The Offertory Sentences
18. The Offertory
19. Doxology
20. Offertory Prayer of Dedication

Act of Renewal:

21. Musical Interlude or Hymn
22. Sermon
23. Invitation to Christian Discipleship
24. Hymn of Invitation and Consecration
25. Communion of the Lord's Supper
26. Benediction
27. Choral Response or Amen
28. Recessional Hymn
29. Organ Postlude.[3]

This order of service, quite detailed, is an elaboration of the orders provided by Foy and by Ainslie and Armstrong. The extra detail fills out the various movements so that each can be fully experienced. There is some variation in where to put the announcements, which, in any case, should be avoided if possible. The order can be changed, though Osborn would want any reordering to conform still to the pattern of worship.[4] The sermon

3. Ibid., 14–19.
4. Ibid., 7.

and the communion belong to the act of renewal, but communion may precede or follow the sermon. If communion does precede the sermon, there should be "nothing between the communion and the sermon except the hymn with which the communion service closes."[5] The better order from Scripture is sermon before communion.[6] The offering should precede the communion always.

The Order of Service for Communion of the Lord's Supper

Two orders of service for the communion in the Lord's Supper are given, one when each member of the congregation participates in the bread and cup as soon as the bread and cup are passed, the other when the congregation participates first in the bread and then in the cup. The order for participation in bread and cup as soon as each is received is as follows:

1. Invitation to the Communion by Minister
2. Hymn for Communion Meditation
3. Opening Communion Sentences by Minister or the presiding Elder
4. Words of Institution for the Bread by Minister or the presiding Elder
5. Prayer of Thanksgiving for the Bread by an Elder
6. Words of Institution for the Cup by Minister or presiding Elder
7. Prayer of Thanksgiving for the Cup by an Elder
8. Communion Hymn
9. The Lord's Prayer by all the people
10. Invitation to Participate by Minister or presiding Elder
11. Bread and Wine passed by Deacons
12. Concluding Communion Sentences by Minister or presiding Elder
13. Communion Hymn
14. Benediction by Minister
15. Choral Response or Amen

5. Ibid., 24.
6. Ainslie and Armstrong, *Book of Christian Worship*, 21; Osborn, *Christian Worship*, 24.

16. Instrumental Postlude.[7]

The other order for communion is simply a rearrangement of the sequence of the above elements. Both orders are much the same as those in the earlier manuals, with a few variations. *Christian Worship* does not include the fraction, as do Foy and Cave, but the four scriptural passages that give the invitation to participate are the scriptural warrant for the breaking of the bread and the pouring of the cup.[8] There is no specific prayer for penitence and confession, as in Cave and in Ainslie and Armstrong, though these ideas may be included in thanksgiving prayers or in the pastoral prayer. The Lord's Prayer has been placed between the prayers of thanksgiving and communion. The communion service is framed with the opening and concluding communion sentences. These Scripture passages are on the theme announced for meditation and form the setting for communion.

The Structure of the Prayers of Thanksgiving

Osborn does not provide any examples of, or commentary on, the prayers of thanksgiving. However they are a vital part of the communion service and central to any effort to examine the theology of Eucharist from a textual perspective. A number of books were written subsequent to Osborn's manual to help elders create appropriate prayers. One of the most influential was *The Elder at the Lord's Table*, by Thomas W. Toler. First released in 1954, it was into its sixteenth printing in 1985. Its specific aim was to help the elders understand and carry out their roles. It includes a collection of fifty-eight prayers of thanksgiving "contributed by elders from more than one hundred churches of the Disciples of Christ,"[9] reflecting some of the variety to be found across the communities. It was prepared with reference to *Christian Worship*.[10]

Osborn's manual was written under the sponsorship, guidance, and review of the Local Church Life Committee of the Home and State Missions Planning Council of the Disciples of Christ. Toler's book was encouraged and reviewed by members of the same committee. With its variety of

---

7. Osborn, *Christian Worship*, 26–28.

8. They are 1 Cor 10:16; 11:26; and 11:23b–25. *Christian Worship: A Service Book*, 501–2.

9. Toler, *Elder*, 59.

10. Ibid., 7.

prayers from across the churches and due to its relationship with the same committee that sponsored Osborn, *The Elder at the Lord's Table* is able to cover areas about which *Christian Worship* has not been specific, especially with regard to the thanksgiving prayers.

It is of the "nature" of these prayers that they are not simply to be read or appear to be taken from a book or other source. Toler would prefer that elders read through the prayers so as to gain "seed thoughts" from which the elder's own prayer could grow.[11] Prayers ought to be brief and limited to the ideas appropriate to the observance of the communion service, though they may include the general theme of the service. They should avoid turning into a pastoral prayer or a sermon.[12] The prayer should contain one or more of the following elements: thanksgiving and gratitude; remembrance for what Jesus has done; recognition of Christ's spiritual presence; petition, especially for the forgiveness of sin; and renewed dedication to Christ. Absent from this list, though present in the prayers of the earlier manuals, are confession and acknowledgment of need, and the invocation of the Spirit.

An analysis of the actual prayers shows that the common elements are found throughout the prayers but not with equal weight. Of the fifty-eight prayers in the book, twenty are single prayers that offer thanksgiving for both bread and cup, while the rest offer thanksgiving for either the bread or the cup. All are addressed to the Father and most conclude "in Jesus' name." The dominant element in the prayers is petition—for cleansing, forgiveness, spiritual help, and discernment of the presence of Christ. Only one prayer does not contain petition. In contrast, eighteen prayers do not contain an explicit thanksgiving, while only a little over half the prayers make a clear reference to remembering some part or aspect of Christ's life. The Holy Spirit is called upon to either guide or dwell in the participants in seventeen prayers.

Almost identical data can be gained from an analysis of the thanksgiving prayers in Carlton C. Bucks's *At the Lord's Table*. Published in 1956, it reprints Toler's prayer outline,[13] and contains seventy-eight prayers from a large number of contributors. There are combined prayers for thanksgiving for bread and cup, and prayers for bread and for cup separately. Almost all are addressed to the Father, though a couple are addressed to Christ and one to the Holy Spirit. Most contain both thanksgiving and petition, but

---

11. Ibid., 59.
12. Ibid., 50–51.
13. Buck, *Lord's Table*, 169.

petition occurs more often and is left out of only two prayers, while ten have no thanksgiving. The petitions ask for help to partake worthily, to live worthily, to discern the Lord's presence, to remember what Christ has done, and to show gratitude. Thanksgiving is for the bread and the cup, for the life and death of Jesus, and for God's gifts. Explicit remembrance and calling to mind of Jesus' actions occurs in only eighteen prayers. The Spirit is called down upon the worshippers in six prayers. Very few prayers contain a confession of sinfulness, though a common petition is that, by partaking of communion, the worshipper may live more worthily.

Toler described the thanksgiving prayer as one that is structured around five elements, but petition and thanksgiving are the dominant elements in the prayers collected by Toler and by Buck. In Buck's collection, the number of prayers without any thanksgiving is significantly greater than the number of those without any petition. The other elements in Buck's thanksgiving prayers—remembrance, recognition of spiritual presence, and renewal of dedication—are present in some prayers. Invocation of the Spirit (on the worshippers only) and acknowledgment of sin and need for assurance are in very few prayers. Nearly all prayers are addressed to the Father and are concluded in Christ's name.

This structure in the thanksgiving prayers parallels that found in the devotional excerpta of Foy, and the thanksgiving prayers in Garrison, Cave, and Ainslie and Armstrong, as well as in Abbott, though the prayers in Toler and in Buck seem to favor petition over thanksgiving. They reflect a definite tradition of worship amongst the Disciples. Its roots lie in the liturgies of Scottish Presbyterianism, which has been recast by the idea of restoring the Supper to its New Testament origins; the desire for simplicity, brevity, and spontaneity in the Supper; and the theological difficulties the church has had with the "unscriptural" doctrine of the Trinity and consequently with the role of the Spirit in the Eucharist.

Conclusion

The orders of service for Sunday morning worship and for communion in the Lord's Supper in *Christian Worship* have their origins in the tradition of the Disciples as reflected in and passed on through the manuals examined in the previous chapter. The structure of the prayers of thanksgiving as found in the collections of Toler and of Buck also reflects this tradition and links the communion service to the liturgies of the Reformed churches.

WATKINS' *THANKFUL PRAISE* (1987)

Thankful Praise contains an order of service; the Common Lectionary proposed by the Consultation on Common Texts in 1983; collections of psalms and responses, prayers, and worship resources for Sunday worship during the different seasons of the liturgical year; and commentary on the resources themselves. It does not intend "to prescribe how all worship should take place in Disciples of Christ congregations," but neither does it intend "simply to reinforce current Disciples practice."[14] Most of the material in the book has been developed "by the writers, as new compositions or as extensively edited resources, in most cases not previously published."[15] A prayer of invitation to the table is taken from *Christian Worship*,[16] and a prayer at the table is taken from Garrison.[17]

Yet *Thankful Praise* is not intended to be merely a new worship manual containing improved prayer forms that differ from current Disciples practice. Its central purpose is "to strengthen Christian public worship and especially the celebration of the Lord's Supper."[18] Five steps are taken in *Thankful Praise* to achieve this purpose. One is to "connect Disciples worship more firmly with the great tradition of Christian worship."[19] A second is to attempt to respond openly to the search for Christian unity and specifically the agreements on liturgy such as *Baptism, Eucharist and Ministry*[20] and the *COCU Consensus*.[21] Both these steps have opened Disciples worship practice to broader and deeper understandings of Christian worship. A third step, however, is to be faithful to the "crucial features of traditional Disciples worship,"[22] especially the role of lay leadership, prayer that is created anew for each celebration, and the preeminent place of the Lord's Supper. Since Christian worship is affected by and itself affects contemporary life, a fourth step is "to be sensitive to essential lessons from contemporary

---

14. Watkins, *Thankful Praise*, 8.

15. Ibid., 11.

16. No. 176 on p. 139.

17. In the Acknowledgments on p. 192 this prayer is listed as no. 181. It should be no.180. It is actually a prayer for use before communion. See Garrison, *Alone with God*, 223–24.

18. Watkins, *Thankful Praise*, 7.

19. Ibid., 8.

20. Hereafter referred to as BEM. See the bibliography for publication details.

21. Edited by Gerald F. Moede. See the bibliography for publication details.

22. Moede, ed., *COCU Consensus*, 8–9.

life."[23] Such lessons include awareness of social injustice and the church's responsibility to address it, and the realization that Christian theology and worship have embodied anti-Jewish teachings, and that the language in the liturgy has left many people feeling excluded from worship. A fifth step is to "enhance the beauty and diversity" of Disciples worship. This is done through the use of language that is "vivid, biblical and felicitous," and by "encouraging variety in the ordering of the service."[24]

These steps are not arbitrary. They are the practical consequences of six convictions or principles that *Thankful Praise* identifies as emerging from the period of liturgical reform, which continues to take place in the Western churches. We will examine each of these convictions and contrast the overall approach in *Thankful Praise* with that used in *Christian Worship*. The *first* conviction is that "authentic worship is rooted in the church's experience of the gospel, especially as it is expressed in the Bible and in the church's living experience through history."[25] Consequently Scripture and "tradition" form an inseparable basis for Disciples worship. To base worship in Scripture is not merely to recall past deeds of God but to encounter the divine presence as operative here and now. The *second* conviction is that "worship is deeply and inevitably theological."[26] The prayer, the order of service as a whole, and the individual parts of the service have theological import. This leads to two questions. Does this act of worship speak the truth about God? Is this act of worship faithful to the will of God? Yet worship is not theology nor is it to be reduced to a single theology.

The *third* conviction is that "the church encompasses significant diversity in the theological positions on which worship is based."[27] In worship a variety of authentic theological traditions are able to exist, uniting worshippers in thankful praise rather than dividing them in mutual suspicion and in theological isolation. One of the constituents of worship, then, is that it express theological concepts and concerns. But worship also expresses the relationship that exists between the worshipping community and its Christian mission. The *fourth* conviction follows from this. It states that "worship is intimately connected with the church's mission, including

23. Ibid., 9.
24. Ibid.
25. Ibid., 17.
26. Ibid.
27. Ibid.

its struggles for peace and justice in the world."[28] Worship is not an event that occurs between an individual and God at specified moments and that is radically disconnected from all other realities. Rather "God is glorified through the lives of Christians in the world, even as those lives are renewed and sustained by coming together and sharing food in worship."[29] However, communal worship must not only strengthen for mission, but must also be informed by the church's mission. Thus as the church seeks to bring about the equal dignity of men and women in society, it will use inclusive language in worship.

The *fifth* conviction gives context to the preceding principles. It states that "while worship involves ideas that are timeless and universal, it should be expressed through the culture of the local worshipping community."[30] In fact such contextualizing inevitably takes place. *Thankful Praise* aims "to encourage this process, while at the same time, insisting that the indigenous elements be carriers of the Gospel that transcends all particular ideas and experiences."[31] Finally, the *sixth* conviction is that "worship should be open to creative transformation and conformed to enduring standards in its meaning and patterns."[32] In worship there is both continuity with the past and creative contemporary expression.

Christian Worship collected, organized, and made available to Disciples communities a variety of liturgical resources and Disciples practices. While it provided a large and accessible number of themes for worship services, it placed the structure of all worship within a general, recognizable pattern that "brings about a satisfying experience of worship."[33] The purpose of *Thankful Praise* is radically different from this. It does not seek simply to provide resources and a new framework for traditional worship: it seeks to reassess and reinterpret Disciples worship, to lead it out from its isolated tradition, and to bring it into dialogue with the whole of Christian tradition, and with the ecumenical movement. As well, it seeks to bring the implications of theology, mission, and enculturation to bear on traditional worship. This is shown very clearly in the attempt by *Thankful Praise* at some retrieval of the ancient anaphoras and of ordained ministry. Substan-

28. Ibid., 18.
29. Ibid., 18–19.
30. Ibid., 19.
31. Ibid.
32. Ibid.
33. Osborn, *Christian Worship*, 3.

NEW INFLUENCES AND SHAPES

tial changes are proposed, yet they are changes that bring Disciples worship more fully into the Christian tradition and the developments in ecumenical discussions.

This can be contrasted with *Christian Worship*, where material from the Christian tradition is included "as a testimony to our desire for the unity of the church."[34] However there is no dialogue with the material, nor any attempt to incorporate Disciples worship into the broader stream of traditional Christian worship. Such usage is merely a well-intentioned borrowing. Disciples worship is not fundamentally challenged by such an approach, but simply enriched through judicious additions. On the other hand, *Thankful Praise* does not seek to enlarge the usual patterns but to fundamentally change them while at the same time remaining faithful to the crucial features of traditional Disciples worship.

The Order of Service

The order for Sunday Service is divided into five sections so as to emphasize the corporate character of worship.[35] Each section contains elements considered essential to the Sunday service (rendered below in *italics*) and other elements. The order of service is as follows:

A. The Community Comes Together to Serve God in Worship:

1. *Gathering of the Community*
2. Opening Music
3. *Greeting*
4. Hymn
5. *Opening Prayer(s)*

B. The Community Proclaims the Word of God:

6. *First Reading from the Bible*
7. Psalm or Other Response
8. *Second Reading from the Bible*
9. Anthem or Other Response

---

34. Ibid., vii.
35. Watkins, *Thankful Praise*, 25.

  10. *Reading from the Gospel*

  11. *Sermon*

 C. The Community Responds to the Word of God:

  12. *Call to Discipleship*

  13. *Hymn*

  14. *Affirmation of Faith*

  15. *Prayers of the People*

 D. The Community Comes Together Around the Lord's Table:

  16. *Invitation to the Lord's Table*

  17. *Offering*

  18. *Prayers at the Table*

  19. *Words of Institution and Breaking of the Bread*

  20. *Lord's Prayer*

  21. *Peace*

  22. *Communion*

  23. *Prayer after Communion*

 E. The Community Goes Forth to Serve God in Mission:

  24. *Hymn*

  25. *Closing Words*

  26. *Closing Music.*[36]

 There are a number of things to note about this order of service. The term "Opening Prayer" replaces Osborn's "Prayer of Invocation," the term "invocation" being here restricted to that part of the communion prayers that invokes the presence of the Spirit. The opening prayer can be accompanied by a prayer of confession, followed by words of assurance. It would be appropriate to have an "exchange of peace" upon saying the words of assurance.

 A prayer of illumination may begin the proclamation of the Word. Usually there are three Scripture lessons. Ordinarily the first is from the

---

36. Ibid., 24–27.

Hebrew Bible and the third from the Gospel. The second comes from another part of the apostolic writings. The sermon immediately follows the Scripture readings. The affirmation of faith may take the form of the Apostles' Creed, Nicene Creed, a contemporary affirmation of faith, or a Scripture text. The prayer of the people can be in the form of the traditional pastoral prayer, a litany, a bidding prayer, a guided meditation, or be made up of short prayers delivered by different members of the congregation.

The elements of communion may be brought to the table with the offering. There is variety in the way communion is distributed. Plates and trays can be either distributed through the congregation with the congregation either communing simultaneously or as the elements are passed, or the members can come forward and receive of a common loaf and cup.

The closing words can combine a benediction with a commission to go forth to do God's work.

The Sources of the Structure of the Sunday Service

Thankful Praise refers to three sources for the structure of the Sunday service and the coming together around the Lord's table contained within it. They are "the great tradition of Christian worship stemming from the time of the apostles and from the church of the first centuries"; the ecumenical agreements on liturgy, especially *Baptism Eucharist and Ministry* and the *COCU Consensus*; and traditional Disciples worship.[37]

The influence of BEM is reflected in two ways. In BEM and *Thankful Praise* the service is an integrated whole, rather than a Sunday worship service that incorporates the Lord's Supper. For BEM, the service is a "eucharistic liturgy" that "is essentially a single whole."[38] The presupposition that runs throughout *Thankful Praise* is "that worship features the proclamation of the Word of God, *followed* by the enacting and embodying of that Word in Holy Communion."[39] As regards the elements that make up the liturgy, there are close parallels between *Thankful Praise* and BEM II, 27. The parallel is not exact, though, with *Thankful Praise* adding the gathering of the community (element 1) and a call to discipleship (element 12), while omitting the consecration of the faithful to God, reference to the communion of

---

37. Ibid., 8–9.
38. BEM II, 27.
39. Watkins, *Thankful Praise*, 20.

saints, and the prayer for the return of the Lord and definitive manifestation of his kingdom.

However it would be an oversimplification to see *Thankful Praise* as influenced by only BEM. The *COCU Consensus*, reflecting the influence of the Reformed liturgies, lists the following elements as part of the celebration of the Lord's Supper:

- taking the bread and cup
- giving thanks over them for God's creation and redemption of the world in Christ
- breaking the bread
- communion in both elements
- recitation of Christ's Words of Institution
- prayer invoking the Holy Spirit.[40]

Thankful Praise differs from this in that it includes memorial of Christ's deeds, and specifies that the invocation of the Spirit is on the loaf, cup, and community. In the communion prayer developed in 1969 by the COCU commission on worship,[41] memorial refers to the Lord's Supper as a memorial of Jesus' sacrifice, and the Spirit is called upon to sanctify the congregation and the whole church.

The response by the Disciples to BEM[42] showed a concern that BEM's list was too detailed, involving elements that may be unnecessary. They affirmed six elements as central to the Lord's Supper:

- the prayer of the people
- the proclamation of the word
- the offering of the gifts
- the unfailing use of the words of institution
- prayer for invocation of the Holy Spirit (*epiclesis*) on the community and the elements

---

40. Moede, *COCU Consensus*, VI, 18.
41. Watkins, *Thankful Praise*, 145–46.
42. Christian Church (Disciples of Christ), "Christian Church (Disciples of Christ)." See the bibliography for publication details. This text was voted on by the general assembly of the Christian Church (Disciples of Christ) in the United States of America and in Canada, Des Moines, IA, 2–7 August 1985.

- receiving the bread and cup.[43]

Thankful Praise differs from this in that it includes prayers of thanksgiving and memorial.

BEM, the Disciples response to BEM, and the *COCU Consensus* bring forward differing emphases and concerns in their attempts to show what should constitute the structure of the Lord's Supper. Clearly there is much common ground. The structure of the Sunday service and the prayers as the community gathers around the table in *Thankful Praise* emerge from this matrix. Its roots lie in the ancient liturgies of the church, the liturgies of the Reformation, and Disciples tradition. *Thankful Praise* can consequently accommodate a variety of forms and expressions, though this leaves it open to a certain amount of inconsistency.

The Structure of the Prayers at the Table

Within the prayers at the table there are a number of fundamental differences from the Disciples practice as presented by Osborn. Through retrieval of the forms of the ancient anaphoras, *Thankful Praise* attempts a far-reaching reinterpretation and reorientation of Disciples eucharistic praying. Consequently it puts forward three forms for the prayers at the table. However they all are made up of the same basic elements. One form, the "historic" form, corresponds with the form that arose "early in the history of the church" and "is continued today in most Catholic and Protestant churches around the world."[44] Its standard components are:

- introductory dialogue (corresponding to the *sursum corda*)
- expression of joyful praise and thanks (corresponding to the preface)
- congregational response (corresponding to the *sanctus*)
- scriptural words of institution
- memorial of Christ's life, death and resurrection
- invocation of the Holy Spirit on loaf, cup and congregation
- doxology and amen.[45]

---

43. Christian Church (Disciples of Christ), "Christian Church (Disciples of Christ)," 117.
44. Ibid., 47.
45. Ibid.

This list is somewhat selective in that it excludes intercession, present in the *Didache*, and offering, present in the *Apostolic Tradition* of Hippolytus. Intercession and offering become components in the East Syrian, West Syrian, Alexandrian, and Roman eucharistic prayer traditions.

The second form of prayer at the communion table is closer to the type of prayer we have seen in Toler and in Buck in that it consists of two separate prayers: one for the loaf and one for the cup. The prayers are short, prepared for the occasion, and developed by the leader.[46] However they consist of three elements: thanksgiving, memorial, and invocation of the Spirit on loaf, cup, and congregation. Petition is absent. *Thankful Praise* states that the *sursum corda* is "always appropriate at the beginning of the communion prayer"[47] and that the "biblical Words of Institution of the Lord's Supper should always be included,"[48] either as the centerpiece of the prayer itself or as part of the fraction. With these two elements added, the content of the two short communion prayers parallels that of the "historic" prayer.

A third form also contains these same elements. It is structured as a responsive prayer in which leader, pastor, and congregation can each have a part.[49] Unlike the "historic" form, the congregation's responses make up quite a large proportion of the prayer itself, often almost a half of it. An example of such a prayer is no. 19 on pp. 52–53 in *Thankful Praise*.

Within these three forms a further variation is possible. There are a number of responsive prayers that can be used to begin the prayer at the table but that conclude with the pastor beginning the words of institution.[50] Because these responsive prayers usually do not contain an invocation of the Spirit, doxology, and sometimes a memorial, it seems that the pastor would continue on with the memorial, invocation, and doxology found in the "historic" form such as that on pages 48–50. In a sense this responsive prayer can be used in place of the *sursum corda*, preface, and *sanctus*.

Are the prayers in *Thankful Praise* actually consistent with the above lists of structures and desired components? In the main the prayers reflect the given structure without appearing artificially regimented. But there are three areas of inconsistency. A number of prayers have no doxology. Usually they are from those patterned on the traditional Disciples prayers for

---

46. Ibid., 50.
47. Ibid., 51.
48. Ibid., 53.
49. Ibid., 52.
50. Among these prayers are no. 27 (p. 62), no. 43 (p. 69), no. 56 (p. 73), no. 57 (p. 74).

loaf and cup;[51] but some are responsive prayers.[52] Similarly a number of prayers have no invocation of the Spirit on loaf, cup, and congregation.[53] The third inconsistency is that some prayers include petition[54] and intercession[55] even though these are not included amongst the standard components of the prayers at the table. In conclusion, the dominant elements are thanksgiving and memorial; the invocation of the Spirit is not always included; and some prayers do contain intercession and petition.

The Role of the Minister and the Elders in the Prayers at the Table

It has been customary in Disciples practice for two elders different from the minister or presiding elder to pray the prayer for loaf and cup. *Thankful Praise* recommends some "enlargement" of the customary practices. The minister should recite the words of institution and there should be added prayers said responsively by congregation and pastor. Among the responsive prayers that have been included, some assign parts to leader, people, and pastor;[56] some to leader and people;[57] and others to pastor and people.[58] There is a movement away from the role of the elder as traditionally understood in Disciples worship, with a corresponding development of the part played by pastor and congregation.

The Sources of the Roles of Minister and Elders in the Prayers at the Table

The change in roles of pastor, elder, and people in *Thankful Praise* is a direct result of COCU and BEM. The COCU documents have consistently

---

51. No. 42 (p. 69), no. 71 (p. 80), no. 72 (p. 81), nos. 130 and 131 (p. 110), no. 180 (p. 140).

52. No. 44 (p. 70), no. 102 (p. 96).

53. No. 42 (p. 69), no. 44 (p. 70), nos. 102 and 103 (p. 96), no. 129 (p. 109), no. 147 (p. 124), no. 180 (p. 140), no. 183 (p. 143).

54. E.g., no. 132 (p. 111).

55. E.g., no. 182 (p. 142).

56. E.g., no. 56 (p. 73), no. 140 (p. 117).

57. E.g., no. 73 (p. 81), no. 132 (p. 111).

58. E.g., no. 19 (p. 51), no. 114 (p. 109), no. 129 (p. 109).

emphasized the role of the minister in the Lord's Supper. The fifth meeting of COCU in 1965 made this clear in *Principles of Church Union*: "the service shall only be celebrated by an ordained presbyter or bishop, although it is desirable that deacons and unordained men and women assist in the service in appropriate ways."[59] This was reiterated in the 1984 document, *In Quest of a Church of Christ Uniting*: "The action is presided over by a bishop or presbyter, and deacons and lay persons assist in appropriate ways."[60] Though the Disciples present at the adjourned session of the fourteenth plenary understood that the intent of chapter 7, paragraph 47, of *In Quest of a Church Uniting* was an effort "to express the inclusion of the Disciples elder as presbyter," nevertheless the Disciples responded that "it is not clear whether the agreement on presidency allows for the continuation of the ministry of eldership."[61] In attempting to affirm the Disciples notion of elder, the COCU consultation has actually challenged it.

While BEM was more indirect, content simply with stating "in most churches, this [eucharistic] presidency is signified by an ordained minister,"[62] the Disciples response to BEM showed an awareness of the need to reevaluate the role of the elder at the Lord's Table: "*BEM* challenges us to discover the place of elders in the understanding of ministry as set forth in ecumenical theological convergence."[63] *Thankful Praise* attempts to respond appropriately to the challenge of COCU and BEM.

CONCLUSION

The contents, order of service, structure of the prayers at the table, and roles given to minister, elder, and people in *Thankful Praise* reflect elements of the Disciples tradition. However this tradition is brought into contact with and critiqued by both the broader tradition of Christian worship and ecumenical conversations. The change and continuity in *Thankful Praise* reflect an attempt to reestablish Disciples worship within the broader framework.

---

59. COCU, "Principles," 58.
60. Moede, *COCU Consensus*, VI, 18.
61. Christian Church (Disciples of Christ), "Response," 237.
62. BEM II, 29.
63. Christian Church (Disciples of Christ), "Christian Church (Disciples of Christ)," 120.

CHAPTER 5

The Theology of the Eucharist

Expressed in the Communion Prayers

CHRISTIAN WORSHIP AND *THANKFUL Praise* provide contrasting theologies of the Eucharist. We will see this in this chapter as we examine the following elements of each manual: its theologies of worship, the theological implications of the structures of its worship service and its communion prayers, the role of the Holy Spirit in its prayers at the table, and its portrayal of the relationship between Eucharist and the ordained ministry. But there are also points of continuity, too, between the two books, as we will see. At the end, I will evaluate the place of the eucharistic theology of *Thankful Praise* within the Disciples and Reformed traditions.

THE THEOLOGIES OF WORSHIP

There are two understandings of the theology of worship uneasily conjoined in *Christian Worship*. In the previous chapter we saw how the two orders of service vary only in minor ways from the orders found in the earlier manuals. At the roots of this general pattern of order lay Campbell's insistence on a simplicity of worship characterized by good order and decency. Such simplicity resulted in fitting worship since it was understood to allow the symbols to influence directly the heart to love more deeply. More elaborate liturgies obscured this process. However the structure of Sunday worship was governed by the scriptural ordinances for worship for the Lord's day.¹ These ordinances set down what was to make up the worship service, but there was no prescribed order. The integrating factor in this worship was that the various parts were divine ordinances, valid in themselves and necessary as part of "the ancient order of things." The Lord's Supper took its place as simply one independent part in the structure of the service for Sunday worship alongside the other parts of worship, such as reading Scripture and teaching. In the manuals the communion service remained a complete action in itself. With the decline of the Restoration principle, the service was united through the use of themes, an approach especially developed in Abbott, and the introduction of a calendar. In *Christian Worship* the integrating factor is the "pattern of worship," a formalized account of the movements in the soul of the worshipper during worship. This is based on a different theology of worship, which we will now examine.

Christian Worship conformed the received order of worship to an overarching "pattern of worship." The focus was on the service as an act of worship. As a result the Lord's Supper was further obscured and the worshipping individual became overly prominent. This concern for the "pattern of worship" arose from a number of studies, in the 1920s and later, on the psychology of Christian worship. From these studies and his own research Osborn put forward his four movements that make up the "definitive cycle [that] is followed each time in the consciousness of the worshipper."² Different writers give different analyses of the pattern. What is important, however, is the theology of worship that underlies them.

At the center of worship are the movements in the heart of the worshipper:

> Having come to the house of God what the worshipper most desires is the sense of God, an awareness of all things. He desires to pass through a door-of-leaving-behind that he may have release from manifoldness and confusion, cares and sins, perplexities, and affairs. He desires to find salvation and integrity, wholeness and strength, a vision of the ineffable and the divine. The service of worship must assist this adventure, must present the reality and mediate the divine.³

---

1. See the section headed "The Place of the Lord's Supper in the Worship of the Lord's Day" in chap. 2, above.

2. Osborn, *Christian Worship*, 3. Osborn acknowledges his sources in a footnote on p. 6. His own doctoral dissertation (Osborn, "Psychology") dealt with this topic.

3. Vogt, *Modern Worship*, 48.

This experience comes not so much through the content of the service but through "the form of worship."[4] This form is not an arbitrary pattern but a fixed pattern that corresponds to the objective pattern of spiritual experience:

> One must suppose that the reliable logic and sequence of religious experience, as it rises to the level of love of God, determines the pattern inevitably. This is not an arbitrary type of literary construction, it is simply a formal transcript of the spiritual life.[5]

The pattern brings an objectivity to worship without removing the "strong strain of spiritual self-consciousness in the true Protestant."[6] The pattern facilitates the awakening of the emotions in worship. The Bible is the source of this pattern. It provides "the most satisfactory description of the soul's movements in worship. In the sixth chapter of Isaiah the prophet described the elemental, authentic, normal movements of the soul before God in the temple."[7]

For Brightman, legitimate worship occurs only when God is experienced. The aim of all worship is "harmony with the Divine Spirit of the universe."[8] God is always responsive; consequently feelings of the unresponsiveness of God are "quite possibly due to demanding that God speak our language rather than his."[9] It is the worshipper who must be open: "worship comes as near to God as the worth of the worshipper's ideals will permit."[10] Worship that does not "reach God" is not "real worship."[11] Heimsath makes the same point: "By its genius worship is conditional upon the vision of God. Unless he 'makes connection' with the Divine, a man has not worshipped, regardless of how expressive the liturgy or fragrant the incense."[12]

In effect, neither Brightman nor Heimsath give much attention to the meaning and role of the congregation. The emphasis is not on the worship by a community but the worship by the individuals who make up a

---

4. Ibid., 13.
5. Sperry, *Reality*, 283.
6. Ibid., 267.
7. Heimsath, *Genius*, 21.
8. Brightman, *Spiritual Life*, 126.
9. Ibid., 129.
10. Ibid., 130.
11. Ibid., 129.
12. Heimsath, *Genius*, 22.

congregation for public worship. Being in a congregation puts limits on the possible "intimacies of private prayer," but can offer "exaltation and release of spiritual resources which are hardly attainable when the soul is alone with God."[13] *Christian Worship* encourages the members of the congregation to be as engaged as possible, collectively, in the service. However, this is so that the services "will fulfil the Christian conception of the priesthood of all believers before God."[14] This same individualism is found in Toler, where it is specifically applied to the Lord's Supper: "To the discerning Protestant . . . the observance of the Lord's Supper is individual and personal."[15]

The Lord's Supper is important in worship as an act of dedication. For Vogt, "the Eucharist is a great celebration because it is a great sacrament of dedication."[16] In *Christian Worship*, communion, as well as the sermon, show forth God's will, and allow the worshipper to share in and identify with God's redemptive mission. This results in the worshipper experiencing a sense of empowerment and an eagerness "to undertake for God the challenging issues of the hour."[17] Sermon and communion may be interchanged, or one or other excluded, without affecting the essential movement of the worship experience.

The theology of worship in *Thankful Praise* profoundly challenges both of these approaches to worship, which constellate around the "pattern of worship" or an individualistic approach. We have seen that, influenced by BEM, the service in *Thankful Praise* is an integrated whole, not a Sunday worship service that necessarily includes an independent unit that centers around the Lord's Supper. The whole of the Sunday service is an integrated action of Word and sacrament: "While the Word addresses the world in many ways it customarily finds expression during worship in the readings from the Bible and in the sermon and it is enacted at the meal at the Lord's table."[18] The table is not an adjunct but is integral to the central act of worship: "the response of thankful praise reaches its climax in the Lord's Supper."[19] Structurally this is a return to the earliest Disciples practice; however, theologically it transcends Alexander Campbell's reliance on

13. Ibid., 19.
14. Osborn, *Christian Worship*, 7.
15. Toler, *Elder*, 21.
16. Vogt, 23.
17. *Christian Worship: A Service Book*, 6.
18. *Thankful Praise*, 34.
19. Ibid., 44.

THE THEOLOGY OF THE EUCHARIST

the Restoration principle and places the Disciples more securely within the broader tradition of Christian worship.

Writers of manuals have felt free to borrow prayers from other Christian traditions,[20] justified on grounds of the Disciples historic interest in ecumenism. *Thankful Praise* allows prayers in their context to be appropriated into Disciples worship. This gives Disciples worship a broader ecumenical base and deepens the concept of churches praying together rather than of different churches using the same prayers.

There are a number of challenges to the theology of worship undergirding the psychology of religion approach. The first is clearly the nature of worship itself. *Thankful Praise* gives a definition of worship: "The term is generally used, however, in a more restricted sense to mean the gathering of a community of believers for a corporate expression of thankful praise."[21] The two essentials of worship are that it is (1) a corporate act of (2) thankful praise. Worship is "essentially corporate thanksgiving and praise offered by sinful and redeemed human beings in response to God's saving revelation."[22] Community and thanksgiving are the twin foci of the book. The entire order of worship is community-oriented. The community gathers, proclaims the Word of God, responds to the Word of God, comes together around the Lord's table, and then goes forth to serve God in mission.[23] Individuals realize their reality as Christians when they gather as a body (the church) in worship. Worship is not a private transaction with God carried out in public.

Consequently the aim of the form of worship is not to give expression and shape to the feelings that arise in the individual worshipper, but to give expression and shape to the meaning and purpose of the community's act, to the "content of the service." The meaning and purpose of worship is to give praise:

---

20. Osborn, *Christian Worship*, vii; Ainslie and Armstrong, *Book of Christian Worship*, 3.
21. Watkins, *Thankful Praise*, 12.
22. Ibid., 20.
23. Ibid., 24–27.

> Thankful praise is the theme of the Christian's life, shining through everything that Christians say and do ... with readings, songs, sermons and prayers, gifts and sacred meals, we exult in the life God gives, adore the One who loves so fully, give thanks for Jesus our Savior and friend, and renew our promise to serve God faithfully.[24]

As the act of praise of the Christian community it encapsulates the whole life of the believer and the community, offering all in thanks to God. Though clearly this can be a time of "respite from the burdens of life," it is not essentially to be understood as Vogt's "release from manifoldness and confusion, cares and sins, perplexities, fatigues and affairs."[25] Nor can worship be used to measure the worshipper's own "connectedness" with God. It is rather the gathering of the community in Christ's name to give thanks for all life, which is given by God and "tempered and redeemed by the surprising presence of the eternal Spirit."[26]

God is active and encountered in the service. The baptized are gathered, and as a community are open in prayer "to the powerful active presence of God."[27] The Word, "the active power by which God accomplishes the Divine purpose," is expressed "in the readings from the Bible and in the sermon, and it is enacted in the meal at the Lord's table."[28] The Spirit is called upon and acts "in bread and wine and the congregation so that the sacrifice of Christ becomes a real part of our lives, a living presence here and now."[29] During the worship of thankful praise, "God takes the life of the community, blesses it with the gift of Christ through the supper, breaks it and gives it for the service of the world."[30]

This theology of worship highlights the importance of the Lord's Supper in the service. The Lord's Supper is not an independent ordinance necessarily incorporated into the service of the Lord's day. Word and sacrament are integrally related and brought to a climax at the table. The prayer addressed to God at the table "is more significant than any other set of

---

24. Ibid., 7.
25. Vogt, *Modern Worship*, 48.
26. Watkins, *Thankful Praise*, 7.
27. Ibid., 32.
28. Ibid., 34.
29. Ibid., 47.
30. Ibid.

words in the service."[31] The service flows from Word to sacrament. This is the context of eucharistic praying.

This theology of worship contrasts strongly with the two found in *Christian Worship*. It does not see the Lord's Supper as an independent ordinance, and hence able to be placed where simplicity and style dictate. Nor does it associate the Lord's table with the "sense of empowerment" the worshipper feels at a particular time in the service, so that it is celebrated in juxtaposition with the sermon, the invitation to discipleship, and the hymn of commitment, as part of an act of renewal.

THE COMPONENTS OF THE COMMUNION SERVICE AND THEIR INTERRELATIONSHIP

The focus of the communion prayer in Toler is quite different from the focus of the communion prayers in *Thankful Praise*. The Lord's Supper is a "commemoration" that centers around the passion. Remembrance is crucial. It is given heightened stimulation at communion:

> It is in the eating of the bread and drinking of the cup that there is brought to the worshipper's mind something that he has read or heard about Jesus and perhaps some personal experience he has had with his Spirit. In imagination he sees an image of the Master. As imagination and memory are stirred, the worshiper thinks of his own life in comparison with the life of Jesus Christ. He is prompted to offer thanksgiving to God and to seek forgiveness for his sin. As he remembers the way Jesus gave his life completely in the service of God and man, the participant in this creative communion experience renews his dedication to the Christian way of life.[32]

The prayers in Toler reflect this. The emblems represent Christ to the mind of the believer. A selection from the prayers brings this out clearly:

> We drink this cup in grateful remembrance of the Son, of his perfect life and his death upon the cross.[33]

> Our loving Father, we praise thee for this opportunity to respond to our Father's request to remember him in the breaking of bread.[34]

---

31. Ibid., 20, 46.
32. Toler, 21.
33. Ibid., 36.
34. Ibid., 66.

> We thank thee for these emblems of his broken body and shed blood which remind us that he gave his life that we may see in him thy love for us.[35]

The warrant for this act of remembrance is the Last Supper itself: "we partake of them remembering that when Jesus instituted the Lord's Supper in the upper room he asked his disciples to eat of the bread and drink of the cup in his memory."[36] The aspect most often remembered is the passion: "We thank thee for the bread which represents the body of our Lord broken cruelly on Calvary."[37] In some prayers other aspects of Jesus' life are remembered: Jesus as "our great Teacher,"[38] as the one who in all things glorified the Father,[39] as the one whose life as a whole is remembered,[40] and whose life expressed the love of the Father.[41] Special Sundays could have a more specific point of remembrance; hence, for Race Relations Sunday, for example: "Let this loaf and cup remind us of him who commanded that his followers should love one another above all things."[42] In some prayers there is no explicit act of remembrance, but simply the statement that the Lord's Supper is a memorial.[43]

Thanksgiving is not at the heart of the prayers in Toler, though it is prominent. Thanksgiving is offered for a variety of things. It is given for redemption in Christ, for life itself, for the fact that the Last Supper and the Lord's table have been left to humanity as a reminder. Similarly thanks is given for the bread and for the cup because they enable the worshipper to remember what Christ has done.

Petition rather than thanksgiving dominates the prayers. Deeply conscious of what God has done, especially in and through the passion, the worshipper recognizes his or her essential dependence on God and is made acutely aware of his or her own needs. Only one prayer does not contain petition.[44] The petitions in the rest of the prayers are for discernment of

---

35. Ibid., 75.
36. Ibid., 74.
37. Ibid., 63.
38. Ibid., 67.
39. Ibid., 69.
40. Ibid., 72.
41. Ibid., 78.
42. Ibid., 84.
43. Ibid., 78, 80, 84.
44. Ibid., 74.

THE THEOLOGY OF THE EUCHARIST

the presence of Christ in the supper,[45] the forgiveness of sins,[46] spiritual guidance,[47] and a greater sense of Christian awareness and fortitude.[48] The role of the Spirit in the prayers will be discussed below.

The use of the words of institution[49] is related to the concept of remembrance. In the two orders of service in *Christian Worship*, the words of institution precede the prayer of thanksgiving for bread and cup and are said by the one presiding rather than by the elder who is to make the thanksgiving prayer. They are the scriptural warrant for the ordinance, and focus the act of remembering on partaking of bread and cup at the Lord's own supper. A number of invitations to participate accompany the texts of the institution. Their theme is the Lord's death.[50]

Christian Worship offers 115 different themes around which a worship service could be planned. These themes are related to the Lord's Supper through the opening and closing sentences, which are said before the words of institution and after communion. They are all scriptural. They envelope the service at the table and tie it to the theme of the worship as a whole. Toler gives eighteen examples of elders' prayers that further link the supper and the theme.[51] Some are seasonal (e.g., Lent, Season after Pentecost); some are associated with the church calendar (e.g., Reformation Sunday, Race Relations Sunday); and others are for special occasions (e.g., baptism, services for shut-ins who are sick).

The focus of the communion prayer in *Thankful Praise* is thanksgiving offered by the community. The concept of remembrance in the prayers is far

---

45. E.g., ibid., 63, 64, 67, 86–87.
46. E.g., ibid., 73, 74, 75.
47. E.g., ibid., 62, 69–70, 77, 86.
48. E.g., ibid., 67, 71, 77, 86–87.
49. Matt 26:27–28, Mark 14:22 and 23–24, Luke 22:19 and 22:20, 17b; 1 Cor 11:23–24 and 25. Osborn, *Christian Worship*, 501–2.
50. They are 1 Cor 10:16; 11:23–25b, and 11:26. Osborn, *Christian Worship*, 501–2.
51. Toler, *Elder*, 83–96.

removed from that of a recalling to consciousness. It is more the biblical concept of remembrance as *anamnesis*. It is "not to be understood only as a mental recollection of an event that happened 'back then' and 'over there,' but as an action whereby the reality of God's saving act is made newly present for each generation."[52] *Anamnesis* takes place in the context of proclamation, thanksgiving, and invocation of the Spirit.[53] It is not related directly to petition as in Toler. Called to mind so as to be make present again at the Eucharist are the "saving acts and presence of Christ,"[54] including creation[55] and salvation history.[56] *Anamnesis* is not always explicit in the prayers. Some prayers include reference to God's saving actions but without a clear introductory "we remember" formula.[57] In some prayers what is remembered is the Last Supper itself.[58] Remembrance as recollection is still present. One prayer calls upon God to "help us remember: Our Savior Jesus, delivered to death."[59]

Anamnesis is related to thanksgiving rather than petition. Thanksgiving is offered to God for salvation in Christ, for salvation history, and for creation. There are instances, however, where thanksgiving is made for the gift of the table itself. Praise is offered "for this bread of communion by which through the power of your Spirit you make present Jesus' own body given for us."[60] Similarly, "Merciful God, we praise you for this cup of blessing which brings us the new life that comes from you."[61] In the prayer for Pentecost thanks is given for the Spirit's presence at the supper: "We give thanks to you, God of power and might, that you send your Spirit to us at this communion table."[62] These acts of thanksgiving for the table are more reminiscent of Toler than of the early liturgies of the Christian tradition.

Petition is not as central in these prayers as in those in Toler. Because the concept of remembrance in *Thankful Praise* is different and the supper

---

52. Watkins, *Thankful Praise*, 46.
53. Ibid.
54. Ibid.; no. 43 (p. 69).
55. Ibid.; no. 43 (p. 69), and no. 73 (p. 81).
56. Ibid.; no. 56 (p. 73).
57. Ibid.; no. 19 (p. 52), nos. 130 and 131 (p. 110), no. 147 (p. 124).
58. Ibid.; no. 40 (p. 117).
59. Ibid.; no. 132 (p. 111).
60. Ibid.; no. 16 (p. 50).
61. Ibid.; no. 17 (p. 50).
62. Ibid.; no. 40 (p. 117).

THE THEOLOGY OF THE EUCHARIST

is seen as essentially a communal action, there is less emphasis on personal unworthiness and forgiveness of sins. Petition is not seen as one of the standard components of the prayers at the table.[63] Prayer for the descent of the Spirit on loaf, cup, and congregation replaces the petition for discernment of the presence of Christ in the supper. However, the petitions, though less important, are not totally unrelated to those in Toler. The vast majority in *Thankful Praise* ask for a deepening of what it is to be a Christian: "Empower us with your Holy Spirit to live the Christian life faithfully and fully."[64] Also common are petitions for unity with Christ: "May this meal become communion with the living Christ and with the people whom Christ loves."[65] These sorts of petitions comprise the bulk of them. There are, besides, some for the needs of the world,[66] for Christian unity,[67] for discernment of the presence of Christ,[68] and for the coming of the kingdom.[69] There are two prayers that leave room for silent intercession and allow for more concrete intercessions for "the world, the universal church and its leaders and the congregation."[70] Though the context of petition in these prayers is quite different from that in Toler, there is not as great a discontinuity in the content of the petitions, with their emphasis on the living of the Christian life and on unity with Christ.

Thankful Praise recommends "that the biblical words of the Lord's Supper . . . always be included."[71] They should be either the centerpiece of the prayer or spoken while the bread is broken. Again the meaning is wider than a recalling to consciousness of a past event. They are the biblical warrant for eucharistic praying. They are to be spoken by an ordained minister. The ordained ministry signifies "the unity and continuity of Christ's church" and through it the congregation is reminded "that it is joined to Christians of all times and places around this holy table."[72] Thus the words of institution not only recall that it was Christ who initiated this prayer, but

---

63. Ibid., 47.
64. Ibid.; no. 15 (p. 51) is one of many examples.
65. Ibid.; no. 71 (p. 80).
66. Ibid.; no. 44 (p. 70), no. 129 (p. 109), no. 102 (p. 96), no. 140 (p. 117).
67. Ibid.; no. 19 (p. 53), no. 144 (p. 120).
68. Ibid.; no. 140 (p. 117), no. 180 (p. 141).
69. Ibid.; no. 19 (p. 53), no. 71 (p. 80), no. 114 (p. 105), no. 180 (p. 141).
70. Ibid.; no. 181 (p. 141), no. 182 (p. 142).
71. Ibid., 53.
72. Ibid., 58 n. 8.

also relate this specific community to all other Christians through history who have gathered around the table. In this sense the words of institution become a focus of the "communion of saints," a theme not very prominent in either *Thankful Praise* or *Christian Worship*.

There is a high degree of integration between all the different parts of the service in *Thankful Praise*. Till now we have examined these prayers at the table in isolation from the other prayers in the text because this provided the most direct comparison with *Christian Worship*. However, all the prayers in *Thankful Praise* unite in offering as a community thankful praise to God. The opening prayers express the communal dimension and sometimes the sacramental.[73] The prayer of confession "is a corporate prayer which acknowledges both individual and corporate transgressions."[74] A number of the responses to the readings from Scripture express communal thanksgiving rather than ask for individual understanding.[75] The prayers of the people are a "*corporate* response [of thanksgiving] to the One who has given us life."[76] The offering can be understood as "both a thankful response to the proclamation of the Word of God and an act of preparation for the Lord's Supper."[77] All the parts of the service connect Word and sacrament through the underlying theme of corporate thankful praise.

It is in the invitation to the table that we meet most often another understanding of the supper that has been prominent in Disciples theology and worship. This is the presence of Christ at the table because he is host:

> Come share the feast.[78]

> Now Christ invites us to this table spread with his body and blood.
> Let us come to this our true home and the reunion which has no ending.[79]

---

73. Ibid.; no.24 (p. 61).
74. Ibid., 33.
75. Ibid.; no. 8 (p. 36), no. 10 (p. 37).
76. Ibid., 41.
77. Ibid., 45. However it does not have to be viewed in relation to communion and can be seen as a response to the Word—see 57 n. 5.
78. Ibid.; no. 55 (p. 73).
79. Ibid.; no. 178 (p. 140).

Christ spreads the feast for you and me. Bring your new wine and
fresh bread. Prepare the table for the living Lord who makes every
meal a sacrament of love.[80]

The theme here is not so much thankful praise as a sharing in the eschatological banquet. It is an interpretation of the communion in the blessed bread and cup rather than of the anamnetic thanksgiving.

While different invitations to the table offer an alternative interpretation of the Supper, the thrust of the whole service, as seen through its parts, is to offer thankful praise as a community through Word and sacrament.

THE ROLE OF THE HOLY SPIRIT IN THE PRAYERS AT THE TABLE

There are important differences between *Christian Worship* and *Thankful Praise* concerning the role of the Holy Spirit in the Eucharist. Belonging to the tradition of "free" worship, the Disciples have held that the Holy Spirit is active in worship. Worship is left "free" precisely to be open to the promptings of the Spirit. However Disciples worship has always sought to balance the spontaneous and the planned, preferring services characterized by good order and quiet manners: "there is no place in a service of worship for that which is not quiet, orderly and reverent."[81] However the "unbiblical" dogma of the Trinity has provided difficulties for the Disciples, and there is no consistent doctrine of the Holy Spirit.[82] Historically the question of the role of the Holy Spirit has been concerned with coming to faith and baptism. Yet, even this has not been a major concern of Disciples writers since the first generation—a situation reflected in *Christian Worship*, which offers alternatives for those congregations that "dislike to use the *Gloria Patri* and the *Doxology* because of their Trinitarian emphasis."[83]

What role does the Holy Spirit play in the Lord's Supper? The outline for the elders' prayer at the table in Toler does not include an *epiclesis*.[84] The communion prayers bear this out. Of the fifty-eight prayers in Toler's book, only seventeen have any reference to the Holy Spirit, and in these the

---

80. Ibid.; no. 179 (p. 140).
81. Osborn, *Christian Worship*, 12.
82. England, "Holy Spirit," 112.
83. Osborn, *Christian Worship: A Service Book*, 15 n. 1.
84. Toler, *Elder*, 53–55.

The Disciples at the Lord's Table

Spirit is not called down upon the bread and wine but upon the members of the congregation for discernment, guidance, and strength. Thus the prayers read: "Let thy spirit guide us . . . that we might rightly discern the true meaning of Christ's broken body upon the cross";[85] "Inspire us by thy Spirit to obey thy laws";[86] "Let thy spirit guide us."[87] Prayer is also made so that the participant in communion may experience the Spirit: "As we take these emblems may we experience an infilling of thy spirit while we dedicate ourselves to thee anew";[88] "As we receive these emblems of the love of our Lord, make us receptive to the incoming of his spirit."[89] The Spirit is called upon to guide the worshipper in living the Christian life and to deepen the worshipper's experience of God in the context of the remembrance of Christ's love for all humanity.

In *Thankful Praise* the role of the Spirit is quite different. As we have noted above, there are a number of prayers that do not contain an *epiclesis* and a number that have no doxology. However, these are exceptions. Both *epiclesis* and doxology are considered as standard components of the communion prayer.[90] The *epiclesis* is an "invocation of the Holy Spirit in which we pray for the presence of God's Spirit on the loaf and cup and on the gathered community."[91] The action of the Spirit is communal, not individualistic. The test of the authenticity of the Spirit is also communal. Worship is authentic to "the degree to which it creates a life of enduring discipleship and a community which gathers together people of different races, cultures, classes and genders, people who have been alienated from one another as at Babel."[92]

The invocation of the Spirit is given a variety of forms in *Thankful Praise*. Where there are separate prayers for bread and cup there can be separate invocations. Hence, in the prayer for the loaf:

> Even more we praise you for this
> bread of communion by which,
> through the power of your Spirit

---

85. Ibid., 62.
86. Ibid., 68.
87. Ibid., 73.
88. Ibid., 82.
89. Ibid., 76.
90. Watkins, *Thankful Praise*, 47.
91. Ibid., 48.
92. Ibid., 115.

THE THEOLOGY OF THE EUCHARIST

> you make present Jesus' own body
> given for us.[93]

And in the prayer for the cup:

> Empower us with your Holy Spirit
> to live the Christian life
> faithfully and fully.[94]

Other sets of prayers are less tentative in their invocations:

> With your Holy Spirit bless this loaf
> Bless this cup with your living Spirit.[95]

However in this set of prayers the Spirit is not called down upon the community.

In the communion prayer for Pentecost Sunday the pastor does not invoke the Spirit but prays in thanks that God has already sent the Spirit onto the people and the elements:

> We give thanks to you, God of power and might,
> that you send your Holy Spirit to us at this
> communion table, animating your people and
> brooding over this bread and wine,
> that we may receive again Christ's own life.[96]

Some communion prayers contain more straightforward invocations:

> We thank you God, Fountain of Life,
> for this bread and cup.
> Grant that by the power of your Holy Spirit
> we who receive them
> may share in the body and blood
> of our Savior Jesus Christ.
> Fill us with this same Spirit
> that we may be given power for our mission
> of witness and service to all people.[97]

If the prayers express a hesitation it is in their form as an invocation rather than in any difficulty with the role of the Spirit in the prayer at the

---

93. Ibid., no. 16 (p. 50).
94. Ibid., no. 17 (p. 51).
95. Ibid., nos. 130 and 131 (p. 110).
96. Ibid., no. 140 (p. 117).
97. Ibid., no. 15 (p. 49).

table. Despite the prayers that have no mention of the Spirit, the invocation of the Spirit is an essential element of the thanksgiving prayer and the Spirit is called down upon bread, wine, and community. This is more specific than the COCU agreements and the 1969 COCU liturgy.[98] It is another example of the way *Thankful Praise* has sought to place Disciples worship within the context of the whole tradition of Christian worship. This action of the Spirit in the Lord's Supper may also prompt further theological discussion among the Disciples and a furthering of the role of the Spirit in worship.[99]

MINISTRY AND EUCHARIST

Thankful Praise, though acknowledging lay leadership as a crucial feature of Disciples worship,[100] has sought changes in the roles of the minister, the elder, and the congregation in worship. These changes are not always consistent. They show a divergence from the way these roles are described in *Christian Worship* and in Toler, and reflect the present confusion in contemporary Disciples thinking on ministry. However these proposed changes also show the way beyond current conceptions toward more ecumenically, historically, and theologically satisfactory models of ministry in worship. I will examine this issue by looking at the functions of ministers, elders, deacons, and congregation in *Christian Worship*, and then place these roles within the context of the historical development of Disciples ministry and the ecumenical movement. Finally I will offer an evaluation of the response of *Thankful Praise*.

In *Christian Worship*, responsibility for the communion of the Lord's Supper is shared between the one presiding, who may be either a minister or an elder, and two elders. The one presiding makes the invitation to communion; reads the passage for the communion meditation, the opening communion sentences, and the words of institution; leads the Our Father; reads the concluding communion sentences; and pronounces the benediction. One of the two elders offers the prayer of thanksgiving for the bread, the other the prayer of thanksgiving for the cup. The deacons serve the congregation, passing the plates and the trays to the people. The congregation is generally passive. The service book does encourage the services to use

98. Ibid., no. 190 (p. 145).

99. *Thankful Praise* itself attempts to open up the theological implications of invoking the Spirit. See Watkins, *Thankful Praise*, 57 n. 7.

100. Ibid., 9.

THE THEOLOGY OF THE EUCHARIST

responsive and unison readings and prayers as much as possible to allow the congregation to fulfill the concept of the priesthood of all believers.[101] The congregation is active in the hymn for communion meditation, the communion hymn, the Lord's Prayer, and in taking communion.

Toler provides a summary of the theology that allows the elder to preside and pray the prayer for loaf and cup. The elders are not clergy but lay leaders. Ministers would not make more appropriate presiders because they are not endowed with any "singular clerical power." They are ministers "because of [their] desire to serve the church wholly and completely and because [they] have been trained for its leadership."[102] It is baptism alone that renders one suitable to preside, or indeed to carry out any Christian duty: "It is the traditional philosophy of the Disciples of Christ that every Christian is equal in the sight of God and man and, if the occasion demands it, can perform any of the duties of the church."[103] The use of lay elders as presiders symbolizes "the equality of all people before the throne of God and that cardinal principle of Protestantism, the priesthood of all believers."[104] More pragmatic reasons also play a part. The greatest benefit of having elders preside is that all congregations can carry out the ordinance of the Lord's Supper independent of the availability of ordained ministers.

The history of ministry in the Disciples is more complicated than Toler's views allow.[105] The concept of the elder is as much due to Alexander Campbell's fierce anticlericalism as it is due to any New Testament structure in need of restoration. However, for Campbell, the elders were called, elected, and ordained by the community. Hence they "were not lay members, but the ordained pastors of the congregation."[106] The rise of a settled and resident ministry brought tensions between the powers of the ordained elders of a community and those of the ordained minister of the community. In time elders were no longer ordained and lost much of their power within the congregation. The office developed into the one Toler describes—an office of elected lay persons who lead the communion service.

---

101. Osborn, *Christian Worship*, 7.
102. Toler, *Elder*, 27.
103. Ibid., 28.
104. Ibid., 29.
105. Some studies of the history of ministry in the Disciples include: Watkins, "Ministers"; Crow, "Ministry"; Williams, "Development of Ministry"; Williams, "Elders"; Duke and Lancaster, "Ministry."
106. Williams, "Development of Ministry," 303.

89

Toler's theological position fails to address some of the questions most central to the meaning of ordained ministry: the representational nature of ministry, and its function in the preservation of the apostolic tradition. Perhaps both have been obscured from the time of Campbell's anticlericalism. Ecumenical dialogue has reopened these questions for the Disciples, especially with regard to the role of the elder in worship.

Thankful Praise attempts to respond to these concerns. Already the Disciples have opened up their offices to both men and women equally and see the "ministry of women as a gift to the church from the Holy Spirit."[107] *Thankful Praise* clarifies the terms "deaconess," "deacon," and the "diaconate." The former ministries of deaconess and deacon have been combined and those who are a part of this ministry are simply called deacons. The ministry mainly involves serving the communion elements to the congregation. The role of the minister has been given renewed emphasis. The words of institution are to be said by the ordained minister.[108] By saying these, the minister is said to "preside" at the table.[109] Responsive communion prayers for pastor and congregation have been written. In them the ordained minister takes the role of main celebrant, and the parts for the congregation bring out their role as "co-celebrants of communion."[110] A number of prayers are provided for elders to offer for loaf and cup, but, given the importance of the words of institution, and that these are to be said by the pastor, now understood as presiding, the elders are not the sole leaders of the communion service, but pastor and elders together are the "leaders of communion."[111]

This is certainly an attempt to go beyond the confining history of anticlericalism and see the ordained minister as both the one who "signifies the unity and continuity of Christ's church," and as one set apart for ministry of Word and sacrament to "represent to the church its own mission and identity."[112] The minister is given a presiding role in the supper and the role of the elder is modified so that the anomaly of having a "lay person preside

---

107. Christian Church (Disciples of Christ), "Christian Church (Disciples of Christ)," 120.

108. Watkins, *Thankful Praise*, 53.

109. Ibid., 21.

110. Ibid., 52.

111. Ibid., 58 n. 8.

112. Ibid.

in order to 'represent the laity' " is removed.[113] The role of the congregation in this prayer is expanded to "bring out more fully the theological meaning of the service and the congregation's role as co-celebrants of communion."[114] This maintains the crucial role of lay leadership in Disciples worship and places it in dynamic balance with the representative nature of the ministry.

The role of the elder must also be placed in the context of Word and sacrament, not in the context of the supper as an independent ordinance. Whoever presides at the table must also have presided at the Word or else the continuity of Word enacted in sacrament is lost.

While *Thankful Praise* has brought to the fore the representative function of the minister and the minister's role as presider over Word and sacrament, it has not avoided the confusion that the Disciples feel at present when examining the roles of ordained minister, lay elder, and congregation.

THE EUCHARISTIC THEOLOGY OF *THANKFUL PRAISE* WITHIN THE REFORMED AND DISCIPLES TRADITIONS

Despite the number and significance of the differences between *Christian Worship* and *Thankful Praise*, the latter remains within the tradition of the Disciples and the broader Reformed tradition of the theology of Eucharist, though it has much to offer both.

It identifies three features as crucial in Disciples tradition: the role of lay leadership, prayer created anew for each liturgy, and the preeminent place of the Lord's Supper. Certainly the relationship between Word and sacrament in *Thankful Praise* has heightened the place of the supper in worship, made it an essential part of a comprehensive and authentic theology of worship, and broadened its ecumenical perspective. The richness of prayer forms has more than allowed for prayer created anew for each liturgy. The role of the laity in worship has been expanded, especially by the use of responsive prayers, but there is still confusion as to the meaning of ordained ministry and its representational function.

There is much that is held in common with the Reformed tradition. The elements considered essential for the prayers at the table are close to those in the COCU documents. Intercession and offering are not included

---

113. Ibid.
114. Ibid., 52.

as essential elements despite their place in some of the earliest examples of eucharistic praying available to us and, consequently, in a number of the eucharistic prayer traditions.[115] Contemporary worship, while attempting to retrieve the tradition, is still suffering from the narrow theological perspectives of the pre-Reformation and Reformation eras. In its practice, however, *Thankful Praise* has included some prayers at the table that contain intercession.

In the Disciples tradition two concepts have been used to understand the presence of Christ. One is that of Christ as host of the table. This has been especially popular with the Disciples because it has allowed them to have an "open" table, since, if Christ is the host and has invited the guests, then no one can bar any Christian from coming to the table. In this understanding the words of institution are not only a warrant but also an invitation. The second concept is the spiritual presence of Christ in eating the bread and drinking the cup. This has led to the importance of discerning the presence of Christ. It is related to the concept of remembrance as recollection. Liturgically the Lord's Supper is a reenactment of the Last Supper, with the fraction being an intense reminder of the brokenness of Christ on the cross. Simplicity in worship is essential to this process.

This form of remembrance is also present in *Thankful Praise*. The fraction remains a vital part of the service and its potential intensity is recognized.[116] There are prayers based in such remembering: "In broken bread we see, sense and symbolize the sacrifices made once for all. In poured out wine we reconsider, recall, and remember the offering Jesus made for us."[117] *Thankful Praise* brings into this tradition two other forms of presence that belong to the earliest traditions of eucharistic prayers. They are *anamnesis* as an action that makes the reality of Jesus' salvific actions present again for each generation, and *epiclesis*, the invoking of the descent of the Spirit upon bread, cup, and community. Both are central to the prayers in *Thankful Praise* but it is important to see that the worship book has retained continuity with remembrance as recollection and with Christ as host. Also relevant here is that a great number of the prayers are scriptural so that the Word, in various forms, is present to the whole of the service. There is no movement

---

115. See the section headed "The Structure of the Prayers at the Table" in the latter part of chap. 4, which deals with *Thankful Praise*.

116. Watkins, *Thankful Praise*, 53.

117. Ibid., no. 101 (p. 95).

THE THEOLOGY OF THE EUCHARIST

toward seeing metaphysical change in the elements. The presidency of an ordained minister for validity is rejected.[118]

CONCLUSION

While *Thankful Praise* belongs to the Disciples and Reformed traditions, it has also extended those traditions. It has placed the Lord's Supper into a eucharistic theology of worship. It is firmly rooted in the ancient Christian tradition, especially with regard to the centrality of thanksgiving, *anamnesis*, *epiclesis*, presidency by an ordained minister, and relationship to mission. The use of the calendar and the Common Lectionary forge stronger links with other Christian churches. Though there is a great distance between *Christian Worship* and *Thankful Praise*, features of the earlier work have been retained. *Thankful Praise* is not simply a liturgical book with a different theology of Eucharist, but a liturgical resource that has attempted to reappropriate the context and form of eucharistic praying into Disciples worship.

---

118. Ibid., 58 n. 8.

CHAPTER 6

Summary and Closing Reflection

WE HAVE EXAMINED THE theology of Eucharist as expressed through the structure and theology of the prayers for the communion service of the Lord's Supper across 150 years or so of Disciples worship, culminating in our noting a contrast between *Christian Worship* (1953) and *Thankful Praise* (1987). To conclude our examination, I offer a summary of the main points on the journey, an evaluation of *Thankful Praise*, and a closing reflection.

THE ORIGINS OF THE DISCIPLES

Historically the union of various groups and congregations seeking to return to the scripturally based "ancient order" of primitive Christianity gave rise to a new church—the Disciples of Christ. Its theological heritage was in the Reformed tradition, coming through Scottish Presbyterianism. It was also directly influenced by the Scottish Independent movements. The Scottish Independents remained within the Reformed tradition, but, reacting against institutionalization within the Presbyterian Church, they rejected the restrictions, credal orthodoxies, strictures, and clericalism of denominations and sought to live as "Christians," with the Bible as their guide in faith and in organization.

Yet this union of the "Disciples" and the "Christians" was not simply a fundamentalist movement. It relied on the philosophy of John Locke to provide a basis for the relationship of revelation, faith, and reason. Revelation came from God through the Scriptures. The Scriptures themselves gave information about God that reason could not attain. Faith assented to these propositions, which formed the first principles of all further reasoning.

The contemporary political climate should also be taken into account. The political philosophy of Locke was very influential in the newly founded United States of America as it formed the basis of Thomas Jefferson's political thought. The people of the frontier, freed from the old constraints, were predisposed for a Christianity that eschewed denominationalism and sectarianism, and that preached a reasoned and biblically based faith.

THE LORD'S SUPPER IN THE THINKING OF ALEXANDER CAMPBELL

Alexander Campbell emerged as the most prominent theologian, writer and publisher, and leader among the early Disciples. In his writings the Lord's Supper is one of the divine ordinances held weekly as part of the worship on the Lord's day. However the supper, as an ordinance, was independent of the other ordinances that made up the worship of the Lord's day. It was the ordinance that focused on the death of Christ. The supper was a divinely sanctioned memorial that brought to the mind of the worshipper the sacrifice of Christ on the cross and, through this recalling to mind, affected the heart of the believer. Campbell emphasized the spiritual presence of Christ, the centrality of communion, and the priesthood of all believers; and he denied that there was any change in the bread and cup. The supper was held weekly, according to the Scriptures. Simplicity of style in worship was itself a New Testament virtue. Structurally the supper was based on the liturgies of Geneva and Westminster, though "restored" so as to bring it into line with the New Testament. Liturgically and theologically Campbell remained within the Reformed tradition as expressed through the ideal of restorationism.

THE LORD'S SUPPER IN THE MANUALS

The production of manuals in the late nineteenth century brought Disciples worship into a new stage of development. The manuals themselves never sought to be definitive. However, they stabilized worship and greatly aided the planning of services. The Lord's Supper remained an independent, though indispensible, unit of worship, focused on recollecting the death of Christ. The structure of the order for the communion service developed into a more or less fixed pattern. Elders presided at the table and created new prayers for bread and cup for each service. However the prayers for the table given in the manuals show that these, too, developed a certain structure, which itself had roots in the earlier Reformed tradition.

The manuals also show a concern for the unity of the service. Two approaches emerge. One is the use of themes. Worship services are planned around a single theme and this theme is connected with the prayers at the table. Though the focus of the table remained the death of Christ, the themes provided a link between the table and the rest of the service. The second approach is the development of a liturgical calendar around which worship could be planned. In practice this was a variation on the use of themes. As the Restoration principle became less viable, the thematic approach brought unity and cohesiveness to the morning worship service.

THE STRUCTURE OF THE COMMUNION SERVICE IN *CHRISTIAN WORSHIP* AND *THANKFUL PRAISE*

Our reflection on the early manuals led to our direct examination of the two texts, *Christian Worship* and *Thankful Praise*, and we saw that the structures for communion at the Lord's table in these texts differ markedly. *Christian Worship* and Toler's *Elder at the Lord's Table* had their origins in the tradition of the Disciples as reflected in the earlier manuals. *Christian Worship* made two contributions to this tradition. First, it carried forward the thematic approach. By providing a large number of prayers for each part of the service indexed according to theme, it enabled a complete service to be conveniently arranged around a single theme. Its second contribution was to relate the order of service to the definite pattern of worship followed in the consciousness of the worshipper.

Thankful Praise sought to enlarge the usual Disciples practice. It attempted to reestablish Disciples worship within the broader framework of traditional Christian eucharistic worship. The text's contents; order of service; structure of the prayers at the table; and roles of minister, elder, and congregation were reshaped with reference to the traditional Christian eucharistic liturgy, BEM, the COCU discussions, and the crucial features of traditional Disciples worship. It produced a liturgical structure centered around the community's act of thankful praise through Word and sacrament.

SUMMARY AND CLOSING REFLECTION

THE THEOLOGY OF EUCHARIST IN THE COMMUNION PRAYERS IN *CHRISTIAN WORSHIP* AND *THANKFUL PRAISE*

In chapter 5 we explored the theology of Eucharist in the communion prayers by examining the theologies of worship present, the theological implications of the structures of the service and the structure of the communion prayers, the role of the Holy Spirit, and the relationship between the Eucharist and the ordained ministry. The theology of Eucharist in *Thankful Praise* was seen to be radically different from that in *Christian Worship*.

In *Christian Worship* there were two theologies of worship. One had its roots in Alexander Campbell's ordinance-based worship. The second, imposed on this first layer, conformed worship to the definite pattern that is followed in the consciousness of the worshipper. The result was an individualistic, highly subjective worship that further obscured the place of the Lord's Supper in worship and greatly restricted the communal dimension of worship. The focus of the communion prayer in Toler is the recalling to mind of the passion and death of Christ. Toler's prayers are dominated by petition rather than thanksgiving. The words of institution are included and the supper is related to the rest of the service through the use of themes. Very little is said about the role of the Spirit in worship. The Spirit inspires worship in the "nonliturgical" churches, but the view that the doctrine of the Trinity is unbiblical meant a number of communities did not use the *Gloria Patri* or the doxology. In the prayers at the table there is no consistent invocation for the descent of the Spirit on loaf, cup, and congregation, but rather there are occasional prayers invoking the descent of the Spirit on the members of the congregation for discernment, guidance, and strength. With regard to the ordained ministry and Eucharist, *Christian Worship* and Toler repeat the then-current structures with either a minister or an elder presiding, elders being responsible for the prayer of thanksgiving for loaf and cup, and the congregation being active through the responsive and unison prayers in the service.

Thankful Praise rejects both the theologies of worship found in *Christian Worship*. The act of worship is an integrated whole. It is a communal act of thanksgiving centered around the Lord's Supper. Through this approach Disciples worship is rescued from its isolated tradition and placed firmly within the broad Christian tradition of eucharistic praying. Consequently the structure of the prayers at the table undergo radical revision.

The Disciples at the Lord's Table

Their focus is thanksgiving. Memorial as a recalling to mind gives way to a more objective *anamnesis*. Petition becomes secondary to thanksgiving, and is not even seen as one of the standard components of the prayer. The role of the Holy Spirit in thanksgiving and *anamnesis* comes to the fore. The Spirit is called to descend upon loaf, cup, and congregation. Both *epiclesis* and doxology are considered standard components of the communion prayer. The relationship between the ordained ministry and the Lord's table is reestablished, and the role of the congregation in the prayers at the table is expanded. But the place of the nonordained elder emerges as an unavoidable and thorny question.

AN EVALUATION OF *THANKFUL PRAISE*

What is the achievement of *Thankful Praise*? In raising this question it is only fair to be clear about the limitations the book imposes upon itself. It makes no attempt to prescribe how all worship should take place, though it does not intend to simply reinforce current Disciples practice. Nor is it an exhaustive compilation of all necessary worship materials. It aims to stimulate reflection and provide models for the development of worship materials. It clearly holds to the Disciples tradition that prayer be created anew for each celebration.

The most immediate achievement of *Thankful Praise* is that it has placed Disciples worship firmly within the great tradition of Christian eucharistic worship. Disciples prayer at the Lord's table had become narrow and introspective. The table had been a central part of the Sunday morning service but the service itself was disjointed. This isolation is broken and unity is restored to the service by the retrieval both of the relationship between Word and sacrament and of the thanksgiving prayer over loaf and cup, which contains thanksgiving, *anamnesis*, *epiclesis*, and doxology. Disciples worship is greatly enriched and its ecumenical potential is broadened. Earlier worship manuals had borrowed prayers from other traditions and from the early Christian liturgies but had had to modify their original understanding. Through *Thankful Praise* the original sense of the prayers may be shared more authentically with other churches. Disciples concern for the table is now given its proper foundational eucharistic framework.

Thankful Praise also seeks to teach. It has clearly laid out the five principles[1] and the six convictions of liturgical renewal[2] that have guided

---

1. Watkins, *Thankful Praise*, 8–9.
2. Ibid., 17–19.

SUMMARY AND CLOSING REFLECTION

the work. These principles relate Disciples worship to the great tradition of Christian worship, the ecumenical agreements on liturgy, the crucial features of Disciples tradition, and the church's mission to respond to contemporary life and injustice; and a final principle advocates enhancing the beauty and diversity of Disciples worship. The convictions relate to understanding worship as an authentic expression of the church's experience of the Gospel that is theologically rich and diverse, intimately connected to mission, expressed in the culture of the community, both open to transformation and able to transform, conformed to enduring standards in its meaning and patterns, and rich in language. The prayers in *Thankful Praise* reflect these principles and convictions. They are contemporary, biblical, and vigorous.

Sensitivity to ecumenical concerns is furthered through the inclusion in an appropriate context of eucharistic prayers from other traditions and the use of the Common Lectionary, and it is furthered through the incorporation of worship into the church calendar.

Thankful Praise offers a host of challenges and theological insights to the Disciples. The retrieval of the *epiclesis* and of doxology signals the re-entry of the Spirit into the life and theology of the church. The book raises in a practical way the questions of ministry, ordination, the place of elders, and the role of the laity. It proposes some alternatives, making the minister presider, increasing the role of the congregation as co-celebrants, and trying to give a different context to the place of the elder. The position taken in *Thankful Praise* remains somewhat ambiguous, however, but it raises the issues and points toward resolution. Perhaps the difficulty will be eventually resolved through a change in practice rather than through a theological analysis of roles and models of ministry.

The retrieval of thanksgiving, *anamnesis*, and *epiclesis* offers promise for a new Disciples theology of the presence of Christ in the Eucharist. In *Christian Worship* the presence of Christ is understood through two concepts: memorial, and Christ as host at his table. When memorial is taken as recollection, it is deemed to fill the heart with love through the remembrance of the crucifixion so that the presence of Christ is felt. Petition is frequently concerned with discerning Christ's presence. The concept of Christ as host identifies the Lord's Supper with the Last Supper. This heightens the worshipper's consciousness of the passion so that the congregation can identify itself with the apostles. However the ministry of the elders and deacons serves to identify the congregation more closely with the early Christian community in Acts as it met for the "breaking of the bread." With the focus in *Thankful*

Praise on thanksgiving over bread and cup, the tendency to identify the Lord's Supper with the Last Supper, however, is diminished. Remembrance as recollection is replaced with *anamnesis*. *Anamnesis* combined with *epiclesis* brings a new understanding of presence: "Our prayer at the communion table is that through the power of the Holy Spirit Christ will become present to us in the breaking of bread and drinking from the cup."[3] This approach to the question of "real presence" is more in line with BEM.

However, *Thankful Praise* could be regarded as inconsistent here. It retains prayers that view memorial as recollection and prayers in which it is possible to equate the Lord's Supper with the Last Supper. These latter occur mainly in prayers of invitation to the table. In the light of BEM they could be taken to interpret the Eucharist as the eschatological meal of the kingdom, partially realized here but to be fulfilled in the final renewal of creation. However, in the light of Disciples tradition, these prayers could be interpreted as identifying the Lord's table with the Last Supper and with memorial as recollection. More clarity is necessary here so that the eschatological metaphor may emerge more forcefully.

We must ask to what extent has *Thankful Praise* retained the Reformation polemic, especially with regard to offering and sacrifice, and intercession? Intercession is omitted from the list of standard components of the "historic" form of the communion prayer despite its presence in the Antiochene, East Syrian, Alexandrian, and Roman eucharistic prayer traditions. It is also constitutive of the Jewish Todah and Birkat Ha-Mazon forms, which provide the liturgical framework of these eucharistic traditions. Nevertheless intercessions are actually present in many of the communion prayers in *Thankful Praise*. Their scope is quite narrow, focusing more on the worshipper than on the needs of the community, church, and world, the coming of the kingdom, and the communion of saints and the remembrance of the dead. In the eucharistic tradition the intercessions have an important ecclesial dimension, directly relating the praying community to mission, to the communion of saints, and to the eschatological banquet. More attention to intercession in *Thankful Praise* would have enabled the communion prayers to be modeled more closely on the ancient eucharistic prayers, improved the present narrow focus in the intercessions that have been included, strengthened Disciples ecclesiology, and taken another step toward going beyond Reformation polemics.

---

3. Ibid., 47.

SUMMARY AND CLOSING REFLECTION

The category of offering and sacrifice is found in the early eucharistic prayer families. The prayers in the *Didache* and the *Apostolic Constitutions*, book 7, do not have a sacrificial motif and, if accepted as eucharistic prayers, show that sacrifice is a later interpretation of the memorial thanksgiving. In the early eucharistic prayer traditions three senses of sacrifice are joined together: the sacrifice of praise and thanksgiving; the offering of bread and wine, over which the thanksgiving is made; and the sacrifce that consists in all that the faithful have offered in conjunction with the eucharistic celebration.[4] *Thankful Praise* omits offering as a standard component of the historic form of eucharistic praying. Again, however, a number of the prayers contain offering. The three senses of sacrifice are operative in these prayers yet with little cohesion or consistency. Various offerings are made: the bread and cup, praise and thanksgiving, praise and gifts (including the money offering), and prayer of petition and praise. In comparison with the early eucharistic tradition the use of sacrifice and offering is both tentative and inconsistent. If it is to be used as a category to interpret the memorial thanksgiving it should be acknowledged as one of the standard components of eucharistic praying and used in all three senses in the prayer to which it is applied. Still, this tentative use of the category of sacrifice is counteracted by the rich *anamnesis* found in the prayers.

Inconsistency is a major, though perhaps not unexpected, criticism of a book such as *Thankful Praise*. We have seen its inconsistency, both in theory and in practice, with regard to petition, and offering and sacrifice. There is also inconsistency in the use of *epiclesis* and doxology. Both are included in the list of standard components and their centrality to eucharistic praying ought not be underestimated. Yet, too many prayers do not contain *epiclesis* or doxology or both. In part this is due to attempts to modify prayer structures that did not contain either, and in part it can be attributed to Disciples historic neglect of the role of the Spirit at the Lord's table. The result is that it leaves a number of texts deficient.

Despite these criticisms, though, *Thankful Praise* is a highly significant text in the life of the Christian Church (Disciples of Christ). Its potential contribution is in three areas. *Liturgically* it has placed Disciples worship firmly within the context of the Christian eucharistic tradition. It has done this using strong prayers set in clearly eucharistic structures, while remaining faithful to crucial features of Disciples worship. *Theologically* it invites the Disciples to deepen and broaden their understanding of the table; of ministry, order and

4. Power, "Anamnesis," 163.

authority; of the Holy Spirit; of real presence; of ecclesiology and mission; and of the relationship of Word and sacrament vis-à-vis the Reformation polemic, especially with regard to sacrifice and offering, and intercession. In *Thankful Praise* worship becomes a locus for theology. *Ecumenically* it contributes significantly to dialogue. The Disciples have long thought that much could be achieved if the churches would gather and share in the breaking of the bread. It has been a hope held with a certain naivety as it ignored the differing context of eucharistic worship in different churches. However, the retrieval of the great tradition of Christian worship in *Thankful Praise* opens the way for the scandal of closed and separated tables to be overcome.

CLOSING REFLECTION

The liturgical practice of the Disciples remains free, yet there are lines of convergence from historical practice that shape how this freedom is taken up and developed. I had hoped in this work to make some of those lines clearer, if only to have them debunked or challenged or changed by differing practices and customs. What is perhaps more important is that we see that the ways of the church communities have biblical, theological, philosophical, and cultural/social roots. The better these roots are understood and grasped, the more the tradition will be free, and the more it will respond to pastoral imperatives and biblical warrant.

The Disciples are also being challenged by the contemporary ecumenical consensus around eucharistic theology, and indeed a deeper sense of sacramentality. This is not at all new to the church, yet the revised understandings of Eucharist and the renewal of practice, Protestant and Catholic alike, are not without their difficulties for the faithful. These will take a long time to germinate, but nevertheless are well and truly present.

Clearly Disciples worship has moved beyond the timeframe of this study, which closed toward the end of the twentieth century with the first serious engagement with the broad Christian renewal movement, a movement in many ways attributable to the Second Vatican Council. Time, prayer, worship, and praxis will further determine the future of this way of Sunday worship, and mark its contribution to an ecumenical Christianity—so cherished an aim of Alexander Campbell and his followers.

Bibliography

Abbott, B. A. *At the Master's Table: A Book for Those Who Participate in the Rite of the Eternal Atonement.* 4th ed. St. Louis: Bethany Press, 1925.
Adams, Harry B. "Worship among Disciples of Christ, 1865–1920." *Mid-Stream* 7 (Summer 1968) 33–49.
Ainslie, Peter, and H. C. Armstrong. *A Book of Christian Worship.* Baltimore: Seminary House, 1923.
Allen, Ronald J., and Keith Watkins, eds. *Thankful Praise: A Resource for Christian Worship.* St. Louis: CBP, 1987.
Baptism, Eucharist and Ministry. Faith and Order Paper No. 111. Geneva: World Council of Churches, 1982.
Barclift, Philip L. "Uniting in Christ at the Lord's Table." *Encounter* 65 (2004) 163–87.
Beazley Jr., George G. "Who Are the Disciples?" *Mid-Stream* 11 (Fall–Winter 1971) 5–82.
Blakemore, W. B. "Worship among Disciples." *Mid-Stream* 11 (Fall–Winter 1971) 116–40.
———. "Worship among Disciples of Christ, 1920–1966." *Mid-Stream* 7 (Summer 1968) 50–65.
———. "Worship and the Lord's Supper." In *The Revival of the Churches*, edited by W. B. Blakemore, 227–52. St. Louis: Bethany, 1963.
Blosser, Joe. "The Table's Edge: Exploring the Historical Boundaries of the Lord's Table in the Christian Church (Disciples of Christ)." *Encounter* 65 (2004) 243–65.
Brightman, Edgar S. *The Spiritual Life.* New York: Abingdon–Cokesbury, 1942.
Brown, Frank Burch. "Style and Substance in Christian Worship." In *Interpreting Disciples: Practical Theology in the Disciples of Christ*, edited by L. Dale Richesin and Larry D. Bouchard, 49–71. Fort Worth: Texas Christian University Press, 1987.
Buck, Carlton C. *At the Lord's Table.* St Louis: Bethany Press, 1956.
Campbell, Alexander, ed. *The Christian Baptist.* Vols. 1–7. Cincinatti, Aug. 3, 1823–July 5, 1830.
———, ed. *The Christian Baptist: Seven Volumes in One.* 13th ed. Revised by D. S. Burnett from Campbell's 2nd ed. Cincinnati, 1861.
———. *The Christian System.* Pittsburg: Forrester & Campbell, 1839.
———, ed. *The Millennial Harbinger*, vols. 1–7, Jan. 4, 1830–Dec. 1836; new series, vols. 1–7, Jan. 1837–Dec. 1843; 3rd series, vols. 1–7, Jan. 1844–Dec. 1850; 4th series, vols.

1–7, Jan. 1851–Dec. 1857; 5th series, vols. 1–7, Jan. 1858–Dec. 1864; vols. 36–41, Jan. 1865–Dec. 1870. Edited with W. K. Pendleton and others, 1846–1866; with W. K. Pendleton and C. L. Loos, 1866–1870. Bethany, VA.

Casey, Michael W. "From British Ciceronianism to American Baconianism: Alexander Campbell as a Case Study of a Shift in Rhetorical Theory." *Southern Communication Journal* 66 (2001) 151–66.

Cave, R. C. *A Manual for Ministers*. Cincinnati: Standard, 1918.

Christian Church (Disciples of Christ), "Christian Church (Disciples of Christ)." In *Churches Respond to BEM: Official Responses to the "Baptism, Eucharist and Ministry" Text, Vol. 1*, edited by Max Thurian, 110–20. Faith and Order Paper No. 129. Geneva: World Council of Churches, 1986.

———, "Response of the Christian Church (Disciples of Christ) to 'In Quest of a Church of Christ Uniting' ", *Mid-Stream* 21 (1982) 227–42.

"Christian Church (Disciples of Christ) in Canada." In *Churches Respond to BEM: Official Responses to the "Baptism, Eucharist and Ministry" Text, Vol. III*, edited by Max Thurian, 264–66. Faith and Order Paper No. 135. Geneva: World Council of Churches, 1987.

Clanton, Caleb J. *The Philosophy of Religion of Alexander Campbell*. Knoxville: University of Tenessee Press, 2013.

COCU (Consultation on Church Union). "Principles of Church Union." *Mid-Stream* 5 (Spring 1965).

Cornwall, Robert D. "The Crisis in Disciples of Christ Ecclesiology: The Search for Identity." *Encounter* 55 (1994) 167–84.

Crow, Paul A. "Ministry and Sacraments in the Christian Church (Disciples of Christ)." *Encounter* 41 (1980) 73–89.

De Groot, A. T. *Disciples Thought: A History*. Fort Worth: Texas Christian University Press, 1965.

Duke, James O. "The Disciples and the Lord's Supper: A Historical Perspective." *Encounter* 50 (Winter 1989) 1–28.

Duke, James O., and Lewis H. Lancaster. "Ministry in the Disciples–Reformed Dialogue." *Mid-Stream* 27 (1988) 109–15.

England, Stephen J. "The Holy Spirit in the Thought and Life of Disciples of Christ." In *The Reformation of Tradition*, edited by Ronald E. Osborn, 111–34. St Louis: Bethany, 1963.

Fikes, Thomas. " 'In a Manner Well Pleasing': The Theology and Practice of the Lord's Supper in the Stone–Campbell Movement, 1800–1875." PhD diss., Fuller Theological Seminary, 2005.

Foy, Jos. H. *The Christian Worker: A Practical Manual for Preachers and Church Officials*. St. Louis: Christian, 1889.

Garrison, J. H. *Alone with God: A Manual of Devotion*. St. Louis: Christian, 1891.

Garrison, Winfred Ernest, and Alfred T. DeGroot. *The Disciples of Christ: A History*. St. Louis: Bethany, 1948.

Green, F. M. *The Christian Minister's Manual: For the Use of Church Officers in the Various Relations of Evangelists, Pastors, Bishops and Deacons*. St Louis: Christian, n.d. [1883?].

Harrison, Richard L. Jr. "Early Disciples Sacramental Theology: Catholic, Reformed and Free." In *Classic Themes of Disciple Theology*, edited by Kennneth Lawrence, 49–100. Fort Worth: Texas Christian University Press, 1986.

———. "Sacraments in the Life, Thought, and Practice of the Disciples of Christ." *Mid-Stream* 27/2 (1988) 94–108.
Heimsath, Charles H. *The Genius of Public Worship*. New York: Scribners, 1944.
Hicks, John Mark. "Churches of Christ and the Lord's Supper: Twentieth-Century Perspectives." *Stone-Campbell Journal* 13 (Fall 2010) 163–76.
Humbert, Harold F. *Worship and the Devotional Life*. Indianapolis: Church Program Planning Committee, Disciples of Christ, n.d.
Lappin, S. S. *Communion Manual: Leader's Edition*. Cincinnati: Standard, 1935.
Lockhart, W. S. *The Ministry of Worship: A Study of the Need, Psychology and Technique of Worship*. St Louis: Christian Board of Publication, 1927.
McAllister, Lester G. *Thomas Campbell: Man of the Book*. St. Louis: Bethany, 1954.
McAllister, Lester G., and William E. Tucker. *Journey in Faith: A History of the Christian Church (Disciples of Christ)*. St. Louis: Bethany, 1975.
McCallum, J. Malcolm. "The Establishing of Historic Christian Worship." *Mid-Stream* 7 (Summer 1968) 66–88.
Moede, Gerald F., ed. *The COCU Consensus: In Quest of a Church Christ Uniting*. New Jersey: Consultation on Church Union, 1984.
Murch, James DeForest. *Christian Minister's Manual*. Cincinnati: Standard, n.d. [1937?].
Osborn, G. Edwin, ed. *Christian Worship: A Service Book*. 2nd ed. St. Louis: Bethany, 1958. First published 1953.
———. "The Psychology of Christian Public Worship." PhD diss., University of Edinburgh, 1935.
Pahl, Irmgard. *Coena Domini I: Die Abendmahlsliturgie der Reformations-kirchen im 16 und 17 Jhd*. Spicilegium Friburgense 29. Freiburg: Universitätsverlag, 1983.
Pearson, Samuel C. "Faith and Reason in Disciples Theology." In *Classic Themes in Disciples Theology*, edited by Kenneth Lawrence, 101–30. Fort Worth: Texas University Press, 1986.
Porter, Calvin L. "Thinking Our Way into the Future with Truth behind Our Backs." *Mid-Stream* 26 (July 1987) 306–16.
Power, David N. "The Anamnesis: Remembering, We Offer." In *New Eucharistic Prayers: An Ecumenical Study of their Development and Structure*, edited by Frank Senn, 146–68. New York: Paulist, 1987.
Short, Howard E. "The Lord's Table: Spiritual Ecumenism." *Mid-Stream* 21 (April 1982) 157–70.
Sikes, Walter W. "Worship among Disciples of Christ, 1809–1865." *Mid-Stream* 7 (Summer 1968) 5–32.
Smith, Benjamin. *A Manual of Forms for Ministers: For Special Occasions and for the Work and Worship of the Church*. St. Louis: Christian Board of Publication, 1928.
Sperry, Willard L. *Reality in Worship: A Study of Public Worship and Private Religion*. New York: Macmillan, 1925.
Spleth, Richard L., and Nancy Brink Spleth. "Contemporary Worship Issues in the Christian Church (Disciples of Christ)." *Mid-Stream* 26 (July 1987) 299–305.
Tappert, T. G., ed. *The Book of Concord: The Confessions of the Evangelical Lutheran Church*. Philadelphia: Fortress, 1978.
Toler, Thomas W. *The Elder at the Lord's Table*. St. Louis: CPB, 1954.
Van Kirk, Hiram. *A History of Theology of the Disciples of Christ*. St. Louis: Christian, 1907.
Vogt, Von Ogden. *Modern Worship*. New Haven: Yale University Press, 1927.

BIBLIOGRAPHY

Watkins, Keith. *The Breaking of Bread: An Approach to Worship for the Christian Churches (Disciples of Christ)*. St. Louis: Bethany, 1966.

———. "The Disciples Heritage in Worship." *Mid-Stream* 26 (July 1987) 291-98.

———. *The Feast of Joy: The Lord's Supper in Free Churches*. St. Louis: Bethany, 1977.

———. *Liturgies at a Time when Cities Burn*. Nashville: Abingdon, 1969.

———. "Ministers and Elders as Leaders of Worship in the Christian Church (Disciples of Christ)." *Encounter* 39 (Summer 1978) 305-20.

———. "Naive Sacramentalism: Barton W. Stone's Sacramental Theology." *Encounter* 49 (1988) 37-51.

———. "Worship in the Christian Church (Disciples of Christ)." *Worship* 51 (November 1977) 486-96.

West, Robert Frederick. *Alexander Campbell and Natural Religion*. New Haven: Yale University Press, 1948.

Williams, D. Newell. "Elders as Assistant Ministers: A Call for Restructure of the Ministry in Congregations of the Christian Church (Disciples of Christ)." *Encounter* 48 (Winter 1987) 93-103.

———. "Historical Development of Ministry among Disciples." *Mid-Stream* 24 (July 1985) 293-315.

Williamson, Clark M. "The Lord's Supper: A Systematic Theological View." *Encounter* 50 (Winter 1989) 47-68.

www.ingramcontent.com/pod-product-compliance
Lightning Source LLC
Chambersburg PA
CBHW050841160426
43192CB00011B/2114